T0002218

What people are say

A Mind Beyond Words

This remarkable book, sharing insights into our innate abilities to communicate with each other and other realms of sentience, beyond the limits of space and time, is a timely contribution to our collective and evolutionary potential and emergent journey. **Dr Jude Currivan,** cosmologist, author, and co-founder of WholeWorld-View

***

A profound story of our intuitive capacity beyond our traditional five senses. *A Mind Beyond Words* is a wake-up call for us to see beyond the surface of our perceptions and judgments of others and ourselves.
Helané Wahbeh, ND, MCR, Director of Research, Institute of Noetic Sciences and President of Parapsychological Association

***

A Mind Beyond Words is a beautiful, touching and enlightening exposition of many of the deeper aspects of life. It gives the reader a tangible sense of levels of reality beyond the material, as well as our innate, natural abilities to access and express our full creative and spiritual potential. This very readable and insightful book is an uplifting guide for anyone who is passionate about exploring the truth about life, spirit and the nature of consciousness.
Pathik Strand, author of *Flowering into Awareness: A Spiritual Manifesto for the 21st Century*

A Mind Beyond Words

My Decades of Discovery with an Extraordinary Guide

A Mind Beyond Words

My Decades of Discovery with an Extraordinary Guide

Jes Kerzen

6TH
BOOKS

Winchester, UK
Washington, USA

JOHN HUNT PUBLISHING

First published by Sixth Books, 2024
Sixth Books is an imprint of John Hunt Publishing Ltd., No. 3 East St., Alresford,
Hampshire SO24 9EE, UK
office@jhpbooks.com
www.johnhuntpublishing.com
www.6th-books.com

For distributor details and how to order please visit the 'Ordering' section on our website.

ISBN: 978 1 80341 534 5
978 1 80341 541 3 (ebook)
Library of Congress Control Number: 2023935094

A CIP catalogue record for this book is available from the British Library.

Design: Lapiz Digital Services

UK: Printed and bound by CPI Group (UK) Ltd, Croydon, CR0 4YY
Printed in North America by CPI GPS partners

We operate a distinctive and ethical publishing philosophy in
all areas of our business, from our global network of authors to
production and worldwide distribution.

To FHB

Contents

Acknowledgements

Although I've told my story with as much authenticity and honesty as I could muster, I'm aware that it is somewhat strange and unconventional. Therefore I'd like to say a special thank you to those precious people who not only believed, but knew this story had to be shared, and encouraged me to get it into print. Those who spring to mind are Cynthia and Bob Dukes and The Council, Cliff Zenker and his lovely family, Susan Snyder, Kate Gannon, Vivien Leyland-Green, Ann and Antony Doveton, Colombe Hudon, Tanya Moore, Angela Rogers and Cheryl Jensen.

Special gratitude goes to Geoff Ward, not only for his meticulous editing and guidance during the drafting process, but also for his support, kindness and advice on how to move the finished manuscript towards the production process.

That leads me on to the team at John Hunt Publishing, who have been patient with my many clueless questions and extremely supportive throughout. In particular I'd like to mention Kristina Kellingley, for having faith in my book from the outset, G.L. Davis, Dominic James, Frank Smecker and Vicky Hartley for her help, kindness and sense of humour.

Finally, of course, I wish to express my everlasting gratitude to 'Asher' for finding me, for guiding me through this incredible journey and for providing the wisdom, thoughts and inspiration that made this book possible. He is an amazing and inspiring person and soul.

First Thoughts

A: I'm thinking.

J: Thinking is silent, but I'm picking up your thoughts. I'm writing with a black pen in a notebook.

A: I can't see what you're writing, but I'm picking up what you write.

J: Weird, isn't it, this telepathy thing?

A: It feels pretty natural though.

J: Yes it does. 150 miles apart, no devices, yet we're having a conversation. It does feel natural, but it's, well, unconventional.

A: That's why you're writing a book about it.

Introduction

This is the story of one of my lives. I have two and they don't mix.

The other life is pleasant enough, but not the kind that deserves to have a book written about it. I suppose I've gone out of my way to keep it as unremarkable as possible. By and large, I've managed to separate these two very different facets of my life quite effectively. What follows, then, will leave the mainstream relationships and experiences aside and focus more or less exclusively on this other, 'secret' life I've been caught up in for the past twenty-five years. Less than a dozen trusted friends have been aware of it. Now you are about to join them.

***

I often wondered, as an increasingly bizarre assortment of events followed one after another, whether we humans have free will, which certainly seems to be the case, or lives governed by some mysterious destiny which, given all those strange synchronicities and twists of fate we encounter, also seems quite plausible. It wasn't until quite recently that a satisfactory answer, one that now seems patently obvious, was presented to me.

The answer came from Asher, who found it in what he refers to as The Realms. Just who Asher is, how we met and how he accesses and relays information to me from these Realms will, I hope, become clear as you read on. For now, though, so that I don't have to resort to using inadequate phrases like 'by a strange coincidence' or 'as if by chance', let me share Ash's explanation of how and why physical lives go the way they do. It's presented, like the First Thoughts above, as I received it, in a telepathic discussion with him.

A: Lives are never random. Each individual has made a plan before starting their physical lifetime. In that planning stage, others have agreed to work with them. It's something like choosing parts in a play. Some may decide to be helpful while others might agree to play the villains in order for the individual to have the life experiences they have chosen to work with. You were told by a channel that you and I had worked together in another life as teacher and pupil and decided to use that role again. That is accurate.

*Our lives are **not** predetermined, though. We all have free choice at every point. This life, for example, might have worked out for either of us in several different ways. It still could.*

*Imagine making the initial plan for a lifetime as setting a destination on a car's satellite navigation system. **Subtle-light navigation**, let's call it 'subt nav', is a system built into the frequency of consciousness, or light, we bring with us into physical life. We have set up an intention for what we want to explore before we begin our journey. Just as sat nav is responsible for finding a route for you, but not for what you decide to do when you get there, so subtle-light navigation will gently direct you to the kind of situation you wanted to find, but will then leave you to gain experience from it in whatever way you choose.*

J: So in a car, sat nav could get me to Brighton, but once there I could decide to shop, go on the pier or sit on the beach. You're saying my 'subt nav' might guide me to the place/time where I could experience a chosen situation: a meeting, a sudden illness or a windfall, for example, but I would have absolute freedom to deal with it in any way.

A: Exactly. For most people the 'subt nav' is extremely subtle. It guides through inspiration, gut feelings, whims, synchronicities and insights. You are gently nudged towards your goal.

J: It occurs to me that at times a vehicle's sat nav is unaware of circumstances down here on the ground. It can't differentiate a smooth route from the roads where residents tend to double park, or those that are full of potholes. Sometimes it tries to send you down a farm track!

A: True. Subt nav also takes little account of the trials and tribulations of everyday life. It knows you asked it to get you to a certain point, so that's what it does. You always have the choice to override it, though, and take a different route.

J: That brings me to my next point, so to speak. What if I consistently ignore the subt nav's promptings and head in a quite different direction?

A: It does what a vehicle's sat nav would do in the same situation. It recalibrates and finds the next-best route. Both are very persistent!

***

Throughout the following pages, I've inserted helpful insights from Asher delivered in this way through our recent telepathic conversations. Unusual, I know, but this life of ours is a very unusual story.

Part I
Asher Watching

Chapter 1

Curious

Miss Robertson's library: that was perhaps my first 'subt nav' nudge — my portal, if I wanted to lend an air of mystery to the whole proceedings. I don't, of course. It's quite mysterious enough without the need for any extra embellishment.

From earliest childhood, and rather to the consternation of my parents, I loved books. People would say things in books they wouldn't dream of saying in real life. Books could transport me to places I hadn't been able to imagine and drip new ideas into my developing mind.

At the age of eleven, when I had worked my way through most of our local library's children's section, I was drawn to meet Miss Robertson. We had recently moved house and she was a new neighbour who kindly invited our family around for afternoon tea. It quickly became clear, from the polite, friendly but rather stilted conversation, that she and my parents had very little in common. She was a slightly bohemian lady, while my parents were not at all of that persuasion. Searching for a topic of conversation, she turned to me and asked what my interests were. When I told her I enjoyed reading, she smiled and suggested that I might like to explore the room on the right at the top of her stairs.

Some time later — probably quite a long time — my mother called up the stairs to ask what I was doing. She had stiffened slightly at the word 'explore' and was clearly concerned that by this time I must surely have broken something; at the very least some law of etiquette. Etiquette mattered a great deal to my mother.

I, meanwhile, was happily perched on a stool in a room filled on all four sides with bookshelves. I was lost in the first volume I'd taken down: *The Time Machine* by H.G. Wells.

"Reading," I called back. "It's wonderful here."

Miss Robertson intervened. "Bring the book down with you, Jessica. You're welcome to borrow it if you'd like to finish it at home."

As I arrived downstairs, she glanced approvingly at my choice.

"Treat that room as your private library," she smiled. "When you've finished that book bring it back and you can choose another. Would you like that?"

***

That was how Miss Robertson's taste in fiction became mine, a passion to study English Literature at school and beyond became inevitable, leading on to a career as a teacher, school librarian and head of English. And that would have been that, had I not, many years later, encountered a boy who rarely bothered to read a book, since he could absorb its contents simply by laying his hand on the front cover for a few moments. Many other events had to fall into place before that, though. First, our paths had to cross and I had to teach him to speak.

***

I was in my mid-thirties before the synchronicities really started to kick in. At that point I was married with three lovely kids and a pet rabbit, living in a dilapidated but interesting Victorian house, which we were doing up in our spare time. I had been on a career break for several years while my children were small and was now doing bits of supply teaching and thinking vaguely about returning to work.

I suppose if you'd pressed me for my favourite book back then I would probably have said either Kahlil Gibran's *The Prophet* or Richard Bach's *Jonathan Livingstone Seagull*, so you could say I had a leaning towards spiritual matters. I still enjoyed science fiction and supernatural tales. Perhaps the word that would best sum up thirty-five-year-old me is *curious*. There were things I was interested to know and understand. I was quite convinced that there were indeed more things in Heaven and earth than my current philosophy encompassed, but I wasn't actively engaged in searching them out.

The next nudge: an old friend phoned one day. She worked in a local school which had a specialist unit for children with speech and language difficulties. She had called to tell me they had a supply teaching post going within the special unit, which would suit me. She was oddly insistent. To this day I can remember her voice on the phone urging and badgering me to contact the head teacher at once. She *knew*, she told me, that I was the right person for this post and anyway, it was only until the end of term...

The truth was, no one else would take it. None of the agency staff or regular supply teachers felt comfortable about trying to teach a bunch of children with little or no spoken language. I have to admit I was hesitant myself. How on earth would I be able to communicate with them, far less deliver the National Curriculum? But then (back to my books) somewhere hidden away in my mind was a memory of reading a biography of Anne Sullivan, Helen Keller's brilliant teacher and mentor. The part where she'd finally managed to get through to the furious and isolated deaf-blind girl, by repeatedly splashing water on her and finger spelling the word 'water' on her hand until Helen made the connection between the two events and understood that she could learn to communicate, had inspired and moved me profoundly. The 'subt nav' was at its most persistent and so, rather nervously, I found myself making an appointment to go and visit.

Unsurprisingly, given the circumstances, I got the job. I found myself working with ten little five- to seven-year-olds with all sorts of problems relating to speaking, understanding and using language. Fascinating! It opened up a whole new world to me; so much more to be curious about.

I met a small girl who answered questions clearly and fluently, but rather strangely at times. She had, it turned out, more-or-less memorised her entire collection of Disney films and used roughly relevant extracts from them as 'scripts' for her spoken language, covering almost perfectly for her own massive difficulties in putting words together.

There was the diplomat's son who had been taken around the world since birth, always cared for by local nannies who chatted and cooed away to him in their own languages. He had reached the age of seven with a cluster of words from various points on the globe and no way of communicating with anyone.

One obviously intelligent little boy was capable only of making vowel sounds. I'll never forget the shock of hearing him read aloud with such perfect intonation, enjoyment and delight that it was clear he understood every word and even the subtlest of jokes, despite only being able to vocalise something like, 'Ee e i-oo uh e-ee oo.'

By the end of the first week I was enchanted. I'd found my perfect job.

What had started as a three-week temporary contract somehow kept extending to become a longer and longer placement and I happily stayed on, and on.

Eventually a day came when I was invited into the head's study after school. She was sitting with the county advisor for speech and language, a wise and perceptive lady who had been tremendously helpful to me during my time with the class. They informed me that the injured teacher I'd been covering for had decided to take early retirement, meaning that the job would now be available as a permanent post.

Eagerly, I asked whether I could apply. By now I had over a term of experience and felt I was beginning to understand how to help these little people develop academically and with their other challenges. The short answer was 'no', although the head assured me that I'd be most welcome to continue as a supply teacher until they found a permanent replacement with suitable qualifications. This specialist post, she explained, needed someone who, as well as having teaching experience, held an additional diploma or degree in speech and language development.

Then the head teacher turned to the county advisor (I'd wondered why she was there!) and they exchanged smiles. She asked whether I would be interested in completing a part-time diploma course while continuing to work in the unit. If so, the permanent job would be mine upon successful completion of the course.

I barely stopped to think. I loved this job. Three children of my own, a full-time job and a distance-learning course? Of course I could do it! There and then I agreed to enrol. This seemed to be the outcome both ladies had been hoping for. Another of my nudges, perhaps...

Much hard work and a few years later I'd received my diploma and enjoyed the experience so much that I'd gone on to study for a postgraduate degree in the subject. I was placed in charge of the whole unit: two classes, each of ten children and with a massive waiting list and had discovered a great deal about how children learn to speak and use language and what to do when, for whatever reason, that doesn't work out well. I knew, without a shadow of a doubt, that this was where I belonged.

***

'When the student is ready, the teacher will appear', or so the saying goes. For me the reverse was true. The teacher was almost ready, so the student decided this would be the right time to put in an appearance.

Just around the time I'd started on my diploma course, a lady across town from where I worked was expecting her first child. It was a difficult birth and although he was an extremely bright little boy and very well cared for, his language skills did not develop as expected. There were problems with the muscles in his mouth, meaning that many speech sounds were hard or impossible for him to produce. In addition to that, though, he struggled to grasp the whole nature of verbal communication.

Asher, the little boy in question of course, tried his best to please adults but made little attempt to engage with other children. The advisory teacher who assessed him in his primary school observed him sitting at a table with other four- and five-year-olds. They were colouring pictures and using a shared pot of crayons. As she watched, the boy slammed his fist down hard on the table and glared at his peers. The other children stiffened and appeared terrified. He then jabbed his finger towards a red crayon on the other side of the table. When a frightened child passed it to him, he wordlessly snatched it and resumed his colouring.

He was, obviously, a prime candidate for one of the places in our unit.

The subtle-light navigation system had done its job; we were destined to meet.

Chapter 2

The Tests

In the five years before arriving in my class, Asher was frustrated and often angry. He simply couldn't comprehend this world he had been dragged into. He could not understand the behaviour or motives of other people, especially the ones his age. They made no sense to him.

He knew, with absolute and unshakeable certainty, that someone was supposed to be there to help.

They'd made that agreement.

He remembered!

He knew it would be a female. She would work with him. She would help him make sense of all this and aid his communication. He assumed she would be one of the 'helpful' people in his life: mother, aunt, nursery assistant? He searched for her constantly and by the age of four, as he sat alone on a bench in the day nursery, watching miserably as the other children went about their shouting and chattering, playing and squabbling, he had started to fear that there had been some dreadful mistake and that she was never going to appear.

He was, though, a deep thinker and a strategist. Despite being a small child with multiple challenges, he set about searching for this elusive helper in a highly original way.

***

Obviously, I knew nothing of that when he arrived in my classroom on a bright, crisp January morning. All I knew was that he had spent four terms in a mainstream school where he hadn't, as his parents and teachers had hoped he would, picked up spoken language or socialisation skills, despite being academically above average. Having read all the paperwork, in which the words 'strong willed' and 'manipulative' appeared fairly often, I was expecting a challenge from this six-year-old and was somewhat surprised, or perhaps lulled into a false sense of security, when he gave me a friendly grin and made a creditable attempt to greet me by name.

Asher, it became apparent over the ensuing weeks, was a child with a formidable intellect, an enhanced sensitivity which made many 'normal' sounds, tastes or smells difficult for him to cope with and a gift for strategy bordering on brilliance. (He was to become the school chess champion at seven, thrashing talented eleven-year-old opponents, and me, with consummate ease.) He was quite a large child for his age with eyes that missed nothing, a smile that could have melted through concrete and barely any comprehensible spoken language.

While he would spend endless hours contemplating life and the cosmos, watching *Star Trek* and devising codes and cyphers, he was baffled by everyday life. He couldn't read facial expressions or tones of voice. He could follow only the simplest of verbal instructions and idiom or sarcasm were lost on him completely.

Yes, of course there was a raft of medical and psychological labels attached to him, then and later, but from my perspective as his teacher, they were of little value. *Dys-this* and *that-ism* merely implied limitations. I was far more interested in what each child *could* do, with the right help and motivation. All our pupils had a complex mix of strengths and challenges and our policy was to read, then put the paperwork aside, watch very carefully, start from where each child was and do all we could to unlock their full potential.

The conditions for learning were favourable: just ten children to a class. As well as myself and a full-time, highly experienced learning support assistant, there was a speech and language therapist who joined us several days each week, so the adult to child ratio was excellent. Having been used to working alone in tough inner city schools with packed classes, control and discipline were certainly the least of my problems here. At least, that had always been the case...

Now, just a few weeks after the start of the term, there came another almost imperceptible nudge. This one was about to set my other, secret, life in motion.

It was nothing I could put my finger on. They were a delightful bunch of children and I prepared each lesson with my usual attention to detail, taking their needs, abilities and interests into account. Somehow, though, I found myself becoming increasingly frustrated. Simply moving around the classroom was difficult. Some child was always under my feet, yet always with a perfectly valid reason for being there. Vital items of equipment, which I *knew* I had laid out ready before taking my lunch break, would inexplicably go missing, only to be found eventually in some ridiculous place by a sharp-eyed child. Listening skills were hugely important, but often now during storytime I'd notice most of the class giggling or mumbling under their breath. In short, a large proportion of my lessons were not going well. It was almost as if someone was sabotaging them.

Slowly, an unlikely but inevitable truth began to dawn. It seemed to have something to do with the new boy: Asher.

I decided to pay him closer attention.

I had a maths lesson planned one day and decided it would provide the perfect chance to watch him. We were doing mental addition, a subject he loved and excelled at. I was writing a number on the board, asking a child to add another number to it and then recording the answer until we reached 100.

There he sat, paying close attention. A few minutes into the lesson, this happened:

"Paul, what's 23 add 8?" I asked.

"31," replied Paul.

I wrote the answer on the board. Asher looked puzzled. "No, it 32," he said, making good use of the few speech sounds at his disposal.

"23 and 8 is 31, Asher," I smiled.

"But you said 23 add 9," he responded. "That 32."

He maintained the poker face — not the slightest smirk curling around his lips. Perhaps he'd made an honest mistake and misheard me. Perhaps not. I pretended to look flustered and apologised, changing the number on the board. Still no hint of a triumphant smile. I was watching very carefully.

We kept going. He would ignore the short easy sums, but when one of the older children was asked to do a more complicated calculation, he would seize his chance. Two or three times more he played a similar trick. I realised why I had been finding lessons so difficult recently. How often had he done such things? More importantly, *why*? He was an industrious little boy, apparently keen to do well and his work was always of a high standard. Was he bored? Was I not stretching him enough academically?

I kept watching for the rest of the week. Yes, *he* was the one who was constantly tripping me up, wherever I needed to be in the classroom. *He* was invariably the one who 'found' the key object that had disappeared before a lesson. *He* was the one who muttered some little catchphrase to the others as they sat on the carpet at storytime, waiting for it to spread and take hold amongst the rest, then sitting back and looking faintly surprised as I remonstrated with my unruly class. *He* was the one drip-feeding misinformation and confusion into so many of my lessons. A six-year-old with a statement of special educational needs had been able to wreck a fair proportion of my classes and waste huge amounts of our time without breaking into a sweat!

When I was absolutely certain, I took him aside one afternoon.

"Asher," I asked, as calmly as I could, "why are you playing these mind games on me?"

This time, I noticed, his mask slipped slightly.

There was a definite glint of excitement as he breathlessly asked, "What do 'mind game' mean?"

"The little tricks you play on me in the classroom," I replied. "All those ways you have of messing up the lessons."

He gave a huge gasp of delight and his eyes were shining. "So it YOU!" he exclaimed. He smiled happily and added quietly, "I thought it wa' you!"

As I sat, completely spellbound, he used the little intelligible language he had to explain the 'tests'. He told me how he had devised them by 'thinking', then tried them out on various people in his life, waiting to find the one who recognised what he was doing. I found myself in the unusual position of being congratulated by a six-year-old child on my achievement — and feeling inexplicably proud!

No, I wasn't exasperated, angry or upset. It never crossed my mind to tell him off or punish him. More than anything, I was in awe of his Machiavellian skills. I'd had many years of teaching experience and met some fascinating children, but nothing had prepared me for Asher. I stared into his eyes and wondered.

Of course *he* knew that something special had happened. He had been planning it for years.

Did I?

I think at some level I recognised it too. I certainly realised that something very unusual and extraordinary had passed between us and I was excited to work with Asher, to get to know him better and to see what would happen next.

***

Half a lifetime later for me, and almost a whole lifetime for him, we are still in touch. As the story unfolds, I hope it will become clear, if it hasn't already, that Asher was, and still is, a highly unusual and fascinating young person.

I will go into far more detail later about the telepathic link we developed while he was still in my class, which has persisted to the present time. For now, let me just share a recent conversation we had, in which he revealed more about his tests:

J: I want to ask you about your early life — before I knew you. Are you able to recall that time and tell me about it?

A: I think so, yes.

J: Did you always know you were going to meet up with me?

*A: I don't remember **not** knowing. I was looking for you and I was cross that it took so long to find you. I was very lost in those years.*

J: So you remembered that before meeting in this life we had made some kind of 'contract'?

A: Yes, I suppose so.

J: What did you remember from it?

A: That you would be a woman and you would be a sort of leader. I knew the person was special and would help me to talk right.

J: But you knew it was more than that? You knew it was reciprocal?

A: Not really. I just knew I needed to find you so I could manage in this world. We'd made a deal.

J: So, you devised your 'tests' to find me and tried them out on various people in your life.

A: Yes.

J: And how old were you when you started using your tests on people?

A: I think I was three or four. I started with Mum but she just got upset and stressed. Then I did it to the ladies at nursery but they didn't get it.

J: So you remembered that 'deal', but I had no idea! I had no recall of it.

A: I know, but you did start to recognise me quite quickly.

Chapter 3

Communicating

There I was in my classroom one lunchtime, quietly preparing the afternoon's lesson, a year or so after Asher had joined us. Suddenly the door burst open and young Max raced in, in great distress.

"Mit, Mit, dum dit!" he cried urgently.

This was Max-speak for 'Miss, Miss, come quick!'

I followed him into the playground, as he did his best to explain that a bunch of big boys had set upon Jimmy. Asher, he told me, had tried to stop them and they had turned their attack on him.

Jimmy was the sort of small, anxious kid who seemed to have a 'victim' sign flashing above his head: an obvious target for bullies. As I arrived at the scene I found one dinner lady leading the weeping child away to be washed and tended, a second berating three sheepish-looking eleven-year-olds and Asher gasping for breath and fighting back tears, standing some way off. I scooped Asher up and led him inside, telling the attackers to report to my classroom at breaktime the next day. Max trotted after us.

Once indoors I checked Asher for injuries, gave him some water and sat him down. He looked scared and confused. He had thrown a few punches during the scuffle and had no idea whether or not I was going to punish him. For all his brilliance in other ways, the child had no way to make any sense of the incident. Asher often needed to have puzzling events explained to him, slowly and in language he could follow.

I delivered the explanation a soundbite at a time, pausing to check he had understood before moving on.

"The big boys were naughty to hurt Jimmy."

Asher's eyes blazed. "He didn't do nothing to them!" he said.

"I know. You saw what happened and you knew it was wrong."

Nod.

"So you went to try to save Jimmy."

Nod.

"There were three of them and they were bigger than you. You were a hero to take them on."

His eyes met mine. He stared in amazement. "You saying I a hero?" he asked tremulously.

"Yes, Asher, I'm saying you were a hero to help Jimmy. But you got hurt, didn't you?"

Nod (but with a huge grin).

"Listen Asher, if big kids do bad things like that again, run very fast and get a dinner lady or a teacher, like Max did."

Nod.

"If you do that, you will be helping but you won't get hurt. Do you understand?"

He thought about it and nodded.

This was the way I gradually helped Asher to make some sense of the world. Such explanations would be required for new and unfamiliar situations for many years to come.

Of course, there were also the speech difficulties. These were the main reason children from our unit were sometimes picked on, teased and bullied by children from the school whose site we shared. Quite a few of them, Jimmy, Max and Asher included, 'talked funny', as the mainstream pupils saw it, due to a condition called oral dyspraxia.

This is how I explained it the next morning to those three bullies:

"I'd like you all to take off one of your shoes. Now take off your sock and put your bare foot flat on the floor."

They glanced at each other, wondering just how unhinged I was. But they knew they'd done wrong, so they did as they were told and waited nervously to see what would happen.

"Now," I continued gently, "I want you to wiggle your middle toe; just the middle one, not any of the others."

One of the boys could just about manage it. The other two couldn't.

"So why can't you two do it?" I asked. "Is it because you're stupid? Are you lazy and not trying hard enough? How come your mate can manage it but you can't?"

The boys looked perplexed. They assured me earnestly that they were trying their best but they could not control the right muscles to achieve it. I turned to their companion.

"How about you? Do you think you're better than your friends? Do you think they're idiots? Are you considering beating them up for being so useless?"

"'Course not," he replied. "It ain't their fault. It don't matter if they can't do it. No one needs to move their toe about anyhow."

I agreed and allowed them to put their socks and shoes back on.

While they were doing so I added, "Ah, but what if the muscles they couldn't control properly were in their mouths? What if they had that sort of difficulty moving their tongues or their lips? Would that matter?"

Realisation was slowly dawning. All three boys were watching me now.

"Quite a few of the children I teach have exactly the same sort of problems two of you just experienced with isolating the right muscles to move their mouths well enough to make speech sounds."

I asked them to make various letter sounds: s, f, t, k, ee, p and so forth, to see how exactly those muscles need to move in order to produce clear speech. In spite of themselves, the boys were becoming interested.

"The children in my class are learning that skill. Every day they have to do exercises to build up muscle strength and control. That's as well as doing all their normal lessons. Gradually they will master new speech sounds and be able to talk more clearly. So do you still think they're stupid or idiots? Do you think they deserve to be teased, imitated, picked on or attacked?"

"No Miss," they said, dutifully.

They felt they'd got off lightly. I hadn't raised my voice, applied any sanctions or made any threats. I felt they'd learned something important and would stop bullying my pupils. We were all correct.

I can't resist adding a postscript to that incident, although it's irrelevant to this story. Knowing that those particular Year 6 boys were keen chess players, I decided to start a school chess club one lunchtime a week. I must confess it gave me the utmost pleasure to watch as little Asher played and beat each of them in turn. Revenge is sweet!

***

Asher's education continued. He made excellent progress, no denying that. He quickly realised that his fellow pupils in the unit were also struggling to master speech and language so began to socialise with them and to form friendships. At the same time, though, he and some of his classmates began showing me other ways of communicating, ways I'd never dreamed of.

One summer afternoon I was at the doorway watching several of the children playing in the class garden. All were aged between five and seven, most had some degree of autistic perception and virtually no intelligible spoken language. Despite that, they were each taking roles within an imaginative game. It had a definite storyline. Each of them knew what to do: when it was time for one person to bring the tricycle taxi to the playhouse door, who was going to ride in it, where they were going and so forth. Small passengers climbed in and out of the taxi, taking turns and never squabbling or fighting for one of the two available seats. No one was visibly organising the activity, yet every child played their part. At first I was simply enjoying seeing them interacting. Then I tried to figure out what was happening.

Was it that they had learned to understand each other's spoken language? No. There was virtually no speech, just laughter, shrieks and sound effects. There was also a great deal of looking. As they watched one another, I realised, they were communicating. I was watching a bunch of little kids engaged in some sort of mind-reading. It wasn't until a year or so later that I appreciated the full significance of that realisation.

***

At around the age of seven or eight, the pupils in my little class who were not yet ready to return to mainstream education moved to our junior class, for a few more years of intensive work on their speech and language skills. A couple of terms after Asher and some of his classmates had made that transfer, a change of teaching staff gave me the option of working in that class, rather than with the infants. I'd always particularly enjoyed teaching seven–eleven year olds and was also delighted to have the opportunity to work with Ash, Max and the others once again.

One day shortly after this transfer, I'd sent the class out to morning break. Most raced outside at once. A single boy hung back until we were alone in the classroom.

"I think," Asher then said to me, rather deferentially, "I should tell you that I'm telepathic."

He waited, a slight smile playing around his lips, for the full impact to sink in.

"You mean you can read my mind?" I asked, suddenly feeling horribly exposed.

He nodded, allowing the smile to break loose.

It may sound odd that a child who had just turned eight should use such a term, with full comprehension, but Ash was, remember, obsessed with *Star Trek*. Looking back, I can see how strongly that programme shaped his outlook and self-image as a young child. Not only did it portray an admirably inclusive culture, in which various humanoid species with very different abilities and characteristics rubbed along fairly comfortably together, it also contained characters Asher could identify with, whether it was Counsellor Troi, with her 'psionic' telepathic abilities or Brett Spiner's brilliantly acted Data, who showed more than a passing resemblance to a person with autistic spectrum perception. ("Yes, Sir. I am attempting to fill a silent moment with non-relevant conversation.") Such depictions of non-standard faculties being accepted and indeed valued would have been extremely comforting to a child who found himself on the fringes of our society.

I didn't doubt that what Asher had told me was true. It actually explained quite a bit. Once again I had the strange feeling that the teacher-pupil role we had was somewhat interchangeable.

Did I wish, somewhere in my mind, that I could learn his skill? Did he pick that thought up and decide to teach me, or was it always part of some grand plan? I suspect the latter.

***

On what started as a very normal Tuesday, my next nudge into strangeness happened. Each child had work to be getting on with in their maths books. Asher was sitting by the window, his seat facing into the room. I had placed myself at a table in the centre of the classroom to help a girl who was struggling to understand fractions. As far as I was aware, I was giving this child my full attention. Behind me, and completely out of my line of vision, Jimmy was standing. Jimmy struggled with almost any independent work. He craved non-stop attention. I can describe what happened next only as an enhanced version of that feeling we all sometimes get when we sense that someone is staring at us, making the hairs rise on the back of our necks or feeling a slight discomfort in the stomach area. My neck was prickling, I felt uncomfortable and I had somehow sensed the reason for this.

Without looking up or turning round, I said, "Jimmy, I'm helping Ellen at the moment. Please stop doing that and wait patiently."

What had happened? Jimmy had not touched me or made any sound. I had simply *known* that he was desperate for help and attention and was becoming very frustrated. I was receiving a very strong sense of his state of mind and it was distracting me.

Asher looked up from his work, took in the situation and let out a yell of delight. "She got it! Well done Jimmy. You did it. Hey everyone, Miss got it!"

The whole class burst into spontaneous applause and I turned round to see Jimmy standing there, maths book in hand, just as, at some level, I had known he would be.

My young pupils were genuinely delighted that I had started to pick up on the secret language they used amongst themselves, while the other adults and I struggled so hard to teach them to talk. I didn't feel comfortable mentioning it to my colleagues or family, though. Already the 'secret life' was beginning. This was kept between the class and myself.

Max was particularly skilled at putting thoughts directly into my mind. During a whole school practice for a harvest festival assembly, several hundred children were crammed into the hot and stuffy school hall. I was on the stage, organising the soloists, having left my learning support assistant to bring our class in. Suddenly I could hear Max's familiar, "Mit, Mit!" urgently in my head.

"Can anyone see Max?" I asked other staff nearby.

It was like searching for a needle in a haystack, but one colleague finally spotted him at the very back of the hall. I left the other teachers to sort out the performers and fought my way through the ranks of restless, sticky children seated on the floor.

Max looked up in relief as I approached.

"What's up?" I asked, as if this were the most natural of occurrences.

Max gestured towards the child next to him. "Ee feel poorly," he said.

Taking one look at the green-faced boy beside him, I swiftly moved him outside into the fresh air and summoned help for him. Disaster averted! Back in the hall, I congratulated Max on his quick thinking.

"OK Mit," he beamed, while silently but clearly acknowledging *my* skill in picking up his message.

***

Asher certainly used this ability from time to time, but not in the same way Max did. I asked him recently why that was the case. His reply (delivered telepathically) surprised me, but made perfect sense.

A: We didn't use it that much then. I would use it to get your attention, then we would use speech. The focus was on getting me to learn to talk and communicate verbally. We were both mainly concentrating on that.

When I asked why he now restricts our 'normal' conversations to the odd word or two on email or social media, his reply was this:

A: Our focus now is no longer on verbal communication. It's on telepathy. So just as it wasn't appropriate to use telepathy when we were working on words, it isn't appropriate to use words now we're working on telepathy.

***

Much as I miss our long, rambling chats (of which more later), I can't fault his logic.

Chapter 4

Nina

By the time Asher had reached the age of eight and been with me in the specialist unit for two years, our respective subtle light navigation systems might appear to have served their purposes. Mine had brought me to a job which broadened my understanding of communication in ways I would never have imagined before, as well as introducing me to Asher and his astonishing group of classmates. His had provided him with the opportunity to begin mastering speech and language, to hone his telepathic abilities with this new group of friends and to locate the 'helper' he had been seeking so diligently.

Before I explain the next part in this story, though, I feel I should add some detail about those 'life plans' Asher mentioned at the start of the book. As I understand it, before becoming incarnate (literally being born in the flesh in 3D life) each of us, as a being of non-physical consciousness, creates the spiritual equivalent of a general plan or design for the life we are about to lead. We decide which issues we wish to address and what aspects of life we would like to be exposed to. These plans involve many others who agree to show up in particular roles, in order to allow us to do this. The point I want to make here is that all the 'bit-part players' in our lives are still pursuing *their own* chosen life paths. Somehow everything meshes together. It sounds like a logistical nightmare from a merely human viewpoint, but I can only assume that working from the perspective of pure overarching consciousness, it has a way of working out.

What follows, then, is a tragedy when looked at in human terms. Despite the suffering and grief it created, though, in a strange way it also played a vital part in strengthening and maintaining the connection between Asher and myself. I wish with all my heart that these things could have happened in a different way, but this is how it played out.

***

Nina was Asher's mum. I warmed to her at once. She was a clever, witty and resourceful lady who loved and cared deeply for her son and was hugely grateful to see his progress as we worked with him in the unit.

In our two tiny classes, with many children staying on for several years, staff developed close links with the pupils' families. There were far more education planning meetings, phone chats and open mornings than in a mainstream school and so I got to know most of the parents very well. With Nina the bond quickly became very strong, but for a heart-breaking reason.

Within a few months of Asher's arrival in the specialist unit and shortly after he had identified me as the helper he'd planned to meet up with, his life took an unexpected turn. Although he wasn't told about it at that stage, his mother was diagnosed with cancer. She went through extensive surgery and then a long and painful course of chemotherapy.

The parents had made the decision not to explain all this to their children, as they were so young. Nina asked me not to discuss it with Asher but to keep a close eye on him, as he was bound to be affected by her frequent hospital visits, weakness and the visible side-effects of the treatment.

She was terribly frightened and often isolated at home by herself in the daytime. Our occasional lunchtime phone calls expanded to several times a week. She needed reassurance that Asher was coping in school, advice on how to deal with some of his behaviour at home and, most of all, someone to listen and care as she shared her fears and pain. I was more than happy to take on that role.

It was often difficult to smile cheerfully and welcome the children back into the classroom after their lunch break, seeing Asher laughing and shouting happily, yet knowing how his mum was suffering and how things were for him at home. I always made sure, though, that I let Nina know about his happy times and successes. She needed all the good news she could get.

No one in school would have known, unless they were watching carefully, that his life had been turned upside down. I noticed only that he spent much more time in silent thought, his head bent and face impassive. I longed to give him the chance to talk, knowing how sensitive he was to the energy of those around him and how often he needed help to understand puzzling events, but I had promised Nina I would stay silent.

It wasn't until she had entered remission and all the treatment had stopped that I said quietly one day, "How's your mummy doing, Ash? She's been rather poorly, hasn't she?"

He looked at me then and his face changed, his eyes wide with fear and horror. Finally he was able to whisper his dreadful secret: "Her hair all gone".

"I know," I confided. "She had to take some medicine to make her better and the silly medicine took her hair away too. It will all grow again soon, now she doesn't need that medicine any more. Think how quick your hair grew back when you had that short haircut in the spring."

I saw a flicker of hope in his eyes. "It going to come back?"

I nodded and smiled reassuringly and he returned to his work.

***

My friendship with Nina continued once she was better. Asher and one of my own children went to the same sports club on Friday evenings and we would sit in the juice bar together chatting cheerfully while our offspring enjoyed their activities.

I suspect that we would have stayed in touch, even after Asher left my class, but life had other plans.

When Asher was eight and a half, Nina's cancer returned. This time it was untreatable. She was given six months to live.

Although Asher says that when he had first devised his 'tests' to find me, he was unaware that there was more than speech and language he would need help with, I can't help believing that my pre-planned role in his life covered considerably more than that. The life path his higher consciousness had chosen was to have far more than its fair share of pain and difficulties.

I did what I could to help his family, taking the boys out at weekends to give the parents some time together or sitting in their home with Nina so that the dad and children could have some afternoons out doing family activities.

Having no experience of supporting a child through bereavement, I approached the staff at the local hospice who gave me masses of valuable advice, as well as a selection of workbooks and colouring sheets I could use. My head teacher agreed to read stories to the class once a week, freeing me to give Asher some individual time to draw pictures, talk through his fears, his nightmares, his frustrations and fury. If we had felt a certain connection before, the changed circumstances meant that an even stronger bond started to form between us. Inasmuch as he could trust anyone in those days when his world was falling apart, Ash trusted me.

I was one of the last of the visitors at the hospice who managed to have a lucid conversation with Nina. I'd been called in urgently after work one evening. She had been asking for me. She was calm and quiet but fully aware of all that was going on. We talked through what was to come. It was an odd conversation. How could it not be? She discussed the funeral plans she had made the way we might once have chatted about a forthcoming holiday. It was so matter-of-fact and so dreadful, all at once.

By now I knew she had no belief in any kind of afterlife, and although she insisted that she would miss her son's smile and cuddling the dog, she also maintained that she'd just go to sleep and cease to exist. I told her I didn't agree, but she brushed my ideas aside.

"I have something to ask you," she said urgently. "I know Ash can't stay in your class forever, but you've become one of his major caregivers and you understand him so well. Can you please stay in touch with him and keep caring and helping him after I've gone, even when you're no longer his teacher? I know it's a lot to ask..."

I assured her that I'd do everything in my power to help and support Asher and that I'd be a lifelong friend to him. She smiled then and relaxed a little, but with so much hurt and longing in her eyes.

"Yes, she said, "I believe you will."

Nina went on to give me instructions on how best to help her husband out with Asher. She knew he would struggle with their son's autistic perception and language difficulties. Finally, she begged me to persuade Asher to go and see her before she passed. He'd been finding visits to the hospice too painful and had stayed away for the last week or so.

"I don't want him to feel bad afterwards, and he will if he leaves it much longer," she said.

That summed Nina up perfectly. To the very end, she was trying to make this horrible situation as easy as possible for those she loved. I promised I'd do my best to persuade Asher and then said a sad and reluctant goodbye to my dear friend.

By the following afternoon she'd closed her eyes, was apparently unresponsive and a day or so later she passed away quietly.

Here, to finish this sad chapter, are Asher's recent thoughts, delivered telepathically, about his mother.

*A: I only shared a life with my mother for nine years. That's a very short time. We had made an agreement, when we made our life plans, that she would leave early. There were several reasons for that. **One** of those reasons was that you and I would get to know each other better and you would have a reason to stay in touch with me, but it also fitted her own plan to have a short life.*

J: It was a terrible loss for you, though.

A: Yes, it was, but it needed to happen. Remember I had chosen to explore many aspects of telepathic communication. She had much to teach us about that.

J: Very true. She did.

***

But that comes a little later in our story.

Chapter 5

The Dialogue Book

During the many months between being told his mother was terminally ill and her actual death, life was unimaginably difficult for Asher. As mentioned before, this was a completely new situation for me as well and I struggled to find ways to help him.

He had a very experienced hospice counsellor, but she had never before worked with a child with the sort of communication challenges Ash presented. The worksheets and colouring pages provided by the hospice were useful to a degree, but while I could see how helpful they would be as conversation starters for many sad and frightened children, they had not been written with neurodiverse thinkers in mind. Autistic perception of the physical world is often very literal, so, for example, when Asher was handed a sheet asking what he wished, he would diligently list all the videos he wanted for Christmas, missing the implied opportunities to explore his wider hopes, dreams and desires. It wasn't that he didn't care about his mother. He cared deeply and desperately. He just didn't process his feelings in the way most people did and he still lacked the verbal ability to try to explain them. There was one deceptively simple device, though, that gave him an outlet for his emotions and a way to explore the thoughts he was wrestling with.

Once they were of an age at which they could read and write independently, I would give every child in my class a dialogue book. The first page always had a 'welcome' card stuck to it, followed by a handwritten message from me, tailored to that child's comprehension level and interests, which asked a couple of questions and invited them to reply. If they wished to read it and respond (that was always optional) they could use 'quiet time' at the start of the school day, while I was marking registers, reading notes from parents and so forth, to do so. There were no rules or restrictions. I made it very clear that spelling and punctuation would not be marked and that they were free to write anything they wished. Once the child had finished, the dialogue book was placed in a sort of dead-letter box, from which I would retrieve it at the end of the day. Overnight, I would read the comments or look at the drawings and write back. The following morning everyone's dialogue book was back in their work tray.

For me it was quite labour-intensive, but the value of helping the children to master the skills of holding a conversation, respond to questions and enjoy a private dialogue with the teacher outweighed any inconveniences.

Some children never touched the books, others wrote only when there was something they particularly wanted to tell me. Asher and a couple of others wrote in theirs every day. I think he was on his sixth book by the time his mother became terminally ill. As the months rolled on and he watched her health gradually decline, his dialogue book became one place where he could safely explore his feelings and attempt to come to terms with the quicksand world he now inhabited.

Mrs Kerzen changes every day.

That was it, stripped down. He accompanied the sentence with a plethora of strange drawings of monsters. They had varying numbers of eyes, limbs and heads and each was labelled with my name.

That, he now saw, was how this world is structured. He sought pattern and order and stability, but they were not to be found. The changes could be almost imperceptible, but sometimes they were massive and catastrophic. School was supposed to be one of the stable parts of his life, but nothing and no one, he was realising, could be relied upon to stay the same. Even this teacher, the one he knew so well and could relate to so easily, was changing by the day. She too would grow older, maybe become ill and at some point she would die or otherwise move out of his life and there would be more parting and more grief.

In his later telepathic communication with me, drawn from his explorations of The Realms, he developed those realisations of his eight-year-old self and framed them thus:

A: Light is total clarity, total brilliance and focus. It is certainty with no room for doubt. That's why it is so hard to convey in a world where duality is in everything. There is light in all people, but always tinged with some shadow, some uncertainty, some doubt. If light is to expand, it must work its way into places where there is shadow and darkness. Physical life is temporary, which means there is what we term 'death', leading to loss and sadness and pain. The body has needs, and the search for fulfilment can become acquisition, greed, conquering or submission. Life on earth is unpredictable. There are many variables and that causes uncertainties and fear. We test ourselves and try to find ways to put more light in place. That just means we are thrusting deeper into the shadows.

***

For his child self, a mother being alive and then dead was total sensory overload. I had no idea how he would cope, or how I could help him through it. In the days after the funeral, I was in close contact with Asher and his family. He asked for another 'secret' outing with me, fearing, I suppose, that now respite care was no longer needed, I might stop taking him out at weekends. We planned a trip to London Zoo for a date some weeks ahead and that became something for him to focus on. It helped, to a degree.

Once he returned to school, the dialogue book became his first port of call. For the first few days he worked in it obsessively. We left him to write and draw for as long as he needed, only gradually encouraging him back into lessons.

Finally, he closed the book and left it for me to read. Although I had learned to expect the unexpected with Asher, I certainly hadn't been prepared for what I was to find there.

First he had drawn a skull and crossbones with the warning, *Be careful I may have some pretty evil plans.*

Over the page he had drawn a highly detailed map. There was a circular road with familiar landmarks; unmistakably the area of our town where the hospice was located. That was, indeed, the only building he had drawn, a long, low structure with double entrance doors. I noticed there was a grid or gate blocking the cul-de-sac in which it was situated. There were arrows leading away from it, along streets he'd labelled with fictitious names such as Tiger Road, Tornado Avenue and even Black Hole. Another gate or grid appeared at the edge of the supermarket car park and from one parking space there was a road leading away, with a bridge crossing the circular road. A 20mph traffic sign indicated the beginning of what was labelled 'motorway'.

For five more pages, this motorway snaked and twisted and zigzagged its way around a convoluted route. The speed limit signs increased exponentially. Gone were the 30mph and 60mph ones he had drawn in the known world. Soon they were up into the thousands. Beside a series of over twenty hairpin bends a dinosaur was lurking. When Asher's route left the motorway to pass through a town, there were dangerous and confusing roundabouts everywhere.

This creation took him hours of painstaking work. I had watched from across the classroom as he bent over the book with total concentration. Clearly it was therapy of some kind.

Back to the map: it wasn't finished yet. Once more the journey joined a motorway. This one doubled backwards and forwards around itself until it passed another hairpin bend at 'Zoop Road', travelling now at two billion miles per hour. Shortly after that the road ceased abruptly at the end of the sixth page. Asher's notes, though, insisted that the following page also constituted part of his map. The image there was of two flat bodies lying on the ground. From each a single pencil line ascended into the air. Towards the top of each, and holding on to its line, was a smiling figure. At first I thought these people were abseiling down towards the bodies. On closer inspection though, I saw that Asher had drawn little dots representing footholds on the parts of the lines between the bodies and the figures. They were moving *up* and away from the flattened shapes below.

At the time, I didn't ask Asher to comment on or explain his picture, realising at some instinctive level that it was the drawing and thought that went into the process which were important. Words were limiting enough for him at the best of times, and this certainly wasn't one of those. As I began writing this chapter, though, I asked whether Ash would be willing to discuss his map with me telepathically, and he agreed to do so.

A: That circular road encapsulated my life at that time. Notice the street names as it approaches the hospice.

J: Yes, they are threatening. The hospice is in a turning off Tornado Avenue. Is that a reflection of how it made you feel to drive along there?

A: Of course.

J: I noticed the two gates on the map. Are they connected in some way?

A: Yes. If you tried to drive to the hospice, you'd be teleported to the car park. There is no way out except on to the motorway. That's the only escape, but it's a trap. You would be driving me in a car and the road is dangerous. You have to drive faster and faster, then we crash at the dead end. On the next page are our bodies but we have left them and we are able to climb free.

J: I'd like to know what your thinking was about death and what happened after it. Where were your smiling people going?

A: My understanding was pretty basic. Dad told me the body would die but the mind would go to Heaven, so that's what I believed.

They are climbing up a beam of light to get to Heaven. It was a good place because you couldn't die there or be ill. I wanted to go there. That's why I planned that journey to the car crash.

J: I see. So we were on a suicide mission. How about 'Zoop Road', though? Its name seemed to link to the journey to London Zoo I'd promised you. I'm picking up some ambiguity there — wanting to die and to live...

A: Exactly right. I was in a polarity.

***

On the ensuing days, Asher used his dialogue book to set me masses of light-hearted puzzles and to ask many questions about the details of the zoo visit; what time we would leave, how much walking would be involved, how we would get from the tube station to the zoo and so on. The suicidal thoughts subsided once he had worked through them in his mind and drawings and he gradually started to readjust to life in a one-parent family.

As for me, the fears and doubts about my ability to support him were very strong at the time. However, I learned a great deal during those months and it served me well as, later in my teaching career, I encountered and worked with several other children dealing with loss and grief.

Naturally, the zoo trip was not our last outing together. In fact, it marked the starting point of the next stage in our secret life.

Part II
Asher Talking

Chapter 6

What's Important Are the Journeys

Of course I did as I'd promised to Nina and continued to support Asher and his father out of school. Both were delighted if I offered to take Ash on trips at weekends or in the school holidays.

As Asher was fully aware, I don't drive, but since our town had a mainline railway station with frequent trains to London, that didn't stop us from travelling. For both of us, those journeys became an opportunity to develop a quite different relationship: a curious mixture of 'unofficial parent' and child friendship and, as the years went by, student and spiritual teacher, with him imperceptibly at first but increasingly taking on the teacher role. I firmly believe this was the start of the real work we had planned to do together in that mysterious 'deal' we struck at some point out of time and space. It was certainly the start of the aspect of my life I couldn't share with my friends or family.

For now, though, Asher was still a little boy. He quickly developed a passion for trains and, in particular, the London tube, or underground system. I'd lived and worked in London for many years when I was younger and knew the network fairly well. On one of our first visits to the capital I presented him with his own tube map and spent the day teaching him how to use it to plan journeys and connections.

As usual, Asher was a fast learner. The map became one of his most treasured possessions and he would spend hours planning our next outing, phoning me in the evenings to announce gleefully that I'd never guess the latest trip he had devised. I would arrive armed with a pair of all-day travel cards, while he clutched a crumpled scrap of paper bearing his secret planned route.

As we rumbled along beneath the streets of London, I'd sometimes try in vain to coax him up into the daylight and fresh air, for a walk across Tower Bridge, perhaps, or a stroll in Green Park, which I would have enjoyed far more. By and large, though, I would let him have his way, appreciating that being in control of these journeys gave him a much-needed antidote to the feelings of powerlessness he'd experienced in the last few years. ("There's nothing that takes your confidence away more than having someone die," he'd told me sadly when he was nine.)

Since the train rides to and from London each lasted an hour or so and our subterranean jaunts took many hours, we spent a great deal of journey time together. I had a small travel chess set, a deck of cards and a few other portable games which helped us to pass the time, but for many of our hours together, we talked. His speech, vocabulary and grasp of the conventions of spoken language had improved tremendously and although there were a few sounds he still couldn't manage and his intonation was slightly stilted, we were able to chat fairly easily. I took the opportunity to teach him jokes, puns and even the beginnings of irony and sarcasm, all of which he would need to understand when he transferred to secondary school. Our conversations, though, became far more than extended lessons. We discovered many interests in common, sharing a deep curiosity about what Douglas Adams termed 'life, the universe and everything' and despite his tender years, he had some quite fascinating theories and insights.

"Where do you get these ideas from?" I remember asking one day, when he was ten or eleven.

"I just *know* some things," he replied, simply. Then he added, rather wistfully, "There's so much in me you *don't* know. You've barely scratched the surface of me."

I thought back over the number of times I had been surprised or even stunned by this young boy and realised that he was right. As I'd first seen when he was a six-year-old, setting tests to find the person who had, at some higher level, agreed to become his helper, Asher was an extraordinary child who probably had at least as much to teach me as I had been able to teach him. I decided to become as diligent a student as I could and was richly rewarded for my efforts.

Here are his recent comments on that conversation.

J: The words you spoke that day have always haunted me. Just how aware were you of the 'hidden realms' in your primary school years?

A: For the first few years in the speech and language unit, my focus was on learning to speak clearly and to understand how communication worked in the physical world. It was very hard work and I was almost exclusively focused on that. I never forgot about The Realms and could still visit them, but I knew I needed these skills to survive independently in this life. By the time I was about eleven, I decided I probably had most of the skills I needed. I suppose I was expecting next to find out how other people experienced The Realms. It came as a shock to realise that they went about their daily lives unaware of them. Even you didn't have much idea. That's what I was thinking when I said that. I realised there was a lot I needed to teach you!

***

There was one particular underground tour when he had factored in only a half-hour stop at our destination, long enough to quickly buy and eat some food. The weather was warm and sunny and I would have liked to explore this part of London. Instead, I was told the journey back was so convoluted that we would need to leave at once if we were to get back to the main rail terminus for our train home.

"Why do you plan our outings like this?" I asked grumpily, as we headed out of the sunlight and back down the steps. "It seems so pointless to spend all that time getting to our destination, only to turn round and head back!"

He stopped and looked at me. "Don't you *see*? Where we end up isn't the part that matters. What's important is the journeys: all the changes and where we go through and the different trains are the main thing." Then he added, "You know that really."

His eyes didn't leave my face until he saw that I'd understood that these journeys of his were a symbol of our lives. Then he nodded, smiled briefly and continued down to the platform.

Recently, he expanded a little on his thinking at that time:

J: Was I right in thinking that you were using it as a metaphor for life?

A: Yes, of course. You got that even then.

J: I can feel there was a grand plan in all that. Can you explain it to me?

A: Well it's fairly obvious really. When I got the tube map and saw how it worked, it felt really familiar. You couldn't remember all your other lifetimes, the journeys we'd been on together, with all the twists and turns and sudden changes of direction. The map showed there were different ways to get to a destination. Some were easy and straightforward and others were really complicated. I always enjoyed the complicated ones.

J: You certainly did! Why was that?

A: They were just more interesting than a simple trip from A to B. There was more jeopardy, more chance it might go wrong, but I'd get a sense of achievement when it all worked out right, like solving a complicated problem. You must share that opinion, or you wouldn't have agreed to take part in so many journeys with me.

J: I assume we're not just talking about tube-train journeys here?

A: Well it's fractal, isn't it? The same thing, but at different scales.

***

So yes, for young Asher, that little London Underground map was a close match to his understanding of the routes one could take, not just through this life, but through the many our souls choose to embark upon.

Chapter 7

My Left Knee

I'm jumping ahead a few years to a time when Asher was in his very early teens and I had returned to mainstream teaching. Our outings continued from time to time, as did our fascinating discussions and the 'knowing' he shared with me. We both had our own separate lives though and for various personal reasons, neither was going particularly smoothly.

I'd reached a point where I'd been feeling very tired and low and, for the first time ever and with great trepidation, I went to see a spiritual healer.

I had no idea what to expect, but he was kind, friendly and put me at ease. I relaxed on his couch and he played quiet, ambient music. I was supposed to drift off into an altered state while he performed the healing.

That was the idea, but it didn't work out that way.

Almost as soon as the therapy started, I felt the most agonising pain coursing through my knee. My whole body jerked with the spasm and it took all my willpower to stop myself yelling out. These jolts of pain, as if I were being gripped by some kind of mechanical vice, continued until he'd finished 'healing' me. The pain only began to subside once he stopped and I could sit up.

The poor man could offer no explanation for what had happened. He mumbled something about me perhaps having a fear of moving forward on my feminine side, but without much conviction. I hobbled from the treatment room, but before I'd reached the end of his road, all trace of discomfort had vanished.

Glutton for punishment, perhaps, but I booked another appointment the following month. Yes, it happened again. I was fine until the healing began and fine afterwards, but during the session I writhed and squirmed and was unable to get any relief.

At that point I gave up on spiritual healing for a while. (Although in all fairness, I must add that once the mystery had been solved, I returned to that healer and had some excellent treatment from him.)

My left knee behaved itself perfectly until a few weeks later when I happened to be listening to a radio programme about séances. Slowly at first, the gripping pain started, gradually becoming more insistent and less bearable. It continued until the programme finished, then stopped completely.

Hmm.

The next day I had time to think things through. Slowly it dawned on me that on each of the three occasions, there had been a connection to things spiritual and 'beyond the veil'. As if in answer to my thoughts, I felt a light but distinct twinge in the knee.

"Keep going," it seemed to be saying. "You're getting there."

Then I had a truly creepy thought. Was someone trying to reach me from *the other side*? The answering twinge was there again. I tried to keep calm. It was fine. Someone 'over there' was mistaking me for some kind of spiritual medium because I'd very occasionally taken an interest in things of a mystical nature. It was obviously a wrong number. After all, who did I know who had passed over and would have any reason to contact me?

Nina?

Ni???

Once more the squeeze but gentle this time — almost a playful nudge.

Nina, known to friends and family by the first syllable of her name, was contacting me.

Knee! More specifically, LEFT knee!

Oh yes, even the sense of humour fitted. She'd been a great Marx Brothers fan…

Ni might have 'left' a few years earlier, but she'd clearly discovered that she was by no means lost in that dreamless sleep she'd been expecting. Our conversation was far from over — in some ways it was just beginning.

I'll leave you to imagine the mix of emotions swirling around in my head at that point. A ghost with a quirky sense of humour could get my attention any time she wanted by applying a vice-like grip to my left knee.

OK.

Well, I'm a pragmatic soul, really, so I decided that (a) she must have a pretty important reason for going to these lengths to get through to me and (b) knowing Nina as I did, it probably had something to do with her beloved family. I therefore decided I'd better find a way of communicating with her; preferably one that didn't involve any more excruciating pressure on my knee.

Clearly my 'subt nav' was working very hard at this time. Was that what had prompted me to go for the healing sessions and to listen to that particular radio show? It surely had to be a nudge in the right direction that I'd recently been reading an article on pendulum dowsing in a magazine; one of those glossy publications aimed at women with an interest in angels, horoscopes and the like. I was, back then, only at the very start of my spiritual journey!

I'd mastered getting my newly acquired crystal pendulum to nod affirmatively backwards and forwards in reply to questions such as, 'Is today Wednesday?' and to shake its little bobbing head from side to side if I asked, 'Am I Mickey Mouse?'

Well it was a start. I figured that if it was that sensitive to 'lie detector' vibrations, she ought to be able to use it to communicate with me.

"Are you Nina?"

Nod, nod, nod went the pendulum, very emphatically.

Whoa.

"Is there something you need to tell me?"

Again, nod, nod, nod.

***

Ah. I'd hit my first snag. The pendulum could only do nod, shake and a manic spinning that seemed to mean I'd confused it utterly. There was no way it could respond to the obvious follow-up question: "What is it?"

So now I had to be a spiritual medium and a mind-reader? The pendulum could deal only with yes/no questions.

"Is it to do with your family?"

Nod, nod, yes.

Right. I had to find a way of narrowing down my questions.

Back to the magazine article. After explaining the lie-detector bit, it had a full page diagram: a circle divided into slices with pictures representing aspects of life the readership might be interested in — travel, romance, home, money and so forth. The idea was to hold the pendulum over the centre of the circle, breathe deeply and become calm and relaxed, ask it what you should focus on in your life and see which section it swung to.

I could adapt this! I grabbed a box of coloured pencils (do ghosts see in colour?) and drew a set of little pictures to stick over the magazine's symbols: her family members, significant others, Nina and myself. This should at least narrow it down a bit. After some thought, I made a second circle with what would now be called emojis: little symbols for happy, sad, worried, help, danger, excited and so on, so she could tell me how she was feeling about these people.

Ni was a quick learner. So was I. Within the space of half an hour, she was communicating with me and my pendulum.

No, she was fine about most things in their lives and various family changes. That was a relief — not a lot I could have done about those.

Next, though, the pendulum veered towards 'danger'.

Danger to...?

It swung to Asher.

Is the danger from someone on the chart?

Nod, nod, nod.

My mouth went dry. I held the pendulum again over the pictures. It swung towards another of the characters I'd drawn: Reece, Asher's new school friend. I knew little of this boy except that, for some reason Asher couldn't fathom, the rest of the class stayed well away from him. Like many children with autistic spectrum perception, Ash had often struggled to get along with his peers. Now, though, he seemed delighted to have found someone who liked and accepted him. He repeatedly told me what a 'laugh' this new best mate was.

I could hardly bear to think of Reece being a danger to Asher, but Nina was adamant. She was even able to use my symbols to show me what the danger was, repeating until I finally grasped her meaning.

As I got the message, the nodding of the pendulum was so strong it was almost wrenched out of my hand.

Next she moved to my little image of myself, then the 'help' icon, then Asher.

Did she want me to speak to her husband or sister about this?

A vehement no.

This, it seemed, was down to me to sort out.

And you know what? It was true.

***

As anyone who has tried to intervene in the social interactions of young teens will know, it involves a great deal of treading on eggshells. After several weeks of gentle and apparently casual probing on my part, Asher admitted that Reece had spent much of his time being temporarily excluded from school for various misdemeanours and had introduced Ash to a group of far older boys. Once I discovered some of the anti-social activities these lads engaged in, I realised that Nina's assessment was true. As in the past, Asher needed help to understand the bigger picture. He had been unable to recognise the dangers inherent in mixing with these young people. Without his mother's warning, I wouldn't have seen what was happening, or been ready to help out when Ash finally agreed that he was out of his depth.

***

Once Reece and his mates had ceased to pose a threat to Asher, I might have expected my communications with Nina to subside. It became apparent, though, that she had another vital message for me.

Initially, our communication was rather stilted, due to the limited range of images I was able to dowse. It quickly occurred to me that if I could dowse symbols, I should be able to use letters of the alphabet to spell out her responses.

"Like some kind of Ouija board," a friend commented after I'd told her the story. Well yes, and it became even more so once I'd drawn myself out an alphabet board and become more skilled at following the pendulum as it wheeled about, stopping and rotating to mark the end of each word.

Did I have doubts about whether this was really happening? Absolutely.

Most of the time, in fact.

I'd often try to find ways of proving to myself that it was genuine. I recall asking about a relative of hers, a lady whose name I'd heard once or twice but couldn't remember. When the crystal swung to spell out the lady's name, I had a 'Yes, of course! ... Oh good grief this is *true!*' moment, but still the doubts wouldn't quite go away.

Something was about to happen, though, that would clear me of any lingering questions about the validity of this extraordinary form of communication. I was about to be given the most incontrovertible proof.

We need to return to Asher. Now in his early teens, the boy was not doing too well. He'd taken his mother's death badly and had been punishing himself for it ever since it had happened. Yes, I know it was from cancer and not in any way his fault, but children have a habit of blaming themselves for all manner of bad things that happen in their lives. This was made worse in Asher's case by the fact that, as mentioned earlier, during her final weeks, he'd been unable to bring himself to speak or respond to his mother at all. Knowing, as a small child, that she was dying, he'd decided to see if he could block her out of his life — a sort of trial run at bereavement.

When I had explained to him, the day after my final meeting with Nina at the hospice, that she was very close to the end of her life and asking to see him, he agreed to go to her and asked his father to take him to the hospice after school so that he could say goodbye and tell her he loved her. Tragically, by the time he got there, she appeared to have sunk into a coma, and was unable to respond to him. He tried again the following morning but there was no change. She died the next day. I'm sure you can imagine the guilt that youngster was carting around with him, believing that his mother died not knowing he loved her.

Now by the time Nina's 'written' messages had started to come through, I'd joined a spiritual development circle and was beginning to take a keen interest in this new life that was opening up before me. After a few weeks, I confided in the group leader, telling her about my contact with Nina and explaining that I wished I could find some way of reassuring her son that he'd done nothing wrong.

"I know she was able to hear him that day," I said. "She literally hung on until he'd felt ready to visit and talk to her, then she left."

"Well, what are you waiting for?" the lady exclaimed. "Don't you see what you can do now? Why do you think you've been *given* this gift, for goodness' sake?"

I listened, dumbfounded, as she explained that I needed to go home, connect with Nina, ask her to dictate everything that had happened on the day her boy had visited, type it out neatly and present it to Asher. This had never occurred to me and to start with I had some resistance to the idea. It was the most private of conversations. I'd feel like an eavesdropper.

Rolling her eyes, my tutor almost pushed me out of the door. "So don't keep a copy! Just write it, seal it in an envelope and put that poor kid out of his misery."

I did exactly as she'd said. The message was incredibly detailed. Nina described everything Asher had said and done. She even spoke of hearing the boy's father knock on the door and ask whether he was okay. We'd never worked on such a long message. When I'd finished, I thanked her, typed it up and sealed it in an envelope, destroying my rough draft.

That weekend, I called Ash and said I had something important to give him. Rather to my surprise, he agreed immediately to meet me, rather than saying he'd be busy with his mates. As gently as I could, I explained the background and the reason his mother and I had made this letter. He was already aware that I had been in contact with his mum. Initially he'd been delighted that there was proof that she was still around but he had never taken much apparent interest in her messages. On this occasion he grinned indulgently.

"What's she been saying now?" he smiled.

I handed him the envelope, telling him to be ready for a shock.

He read it through carefully. Then he turned aside.

I will never forget the look on that young boy's face. I know his life changed on that day, and so did mine.

Chapter 8

Further Afield

By this point, I was definitely living two separate lives. Asher, of course, always had been. We both had our respective family and school worlds to negotiate our way through and to keep as 'normal' as possible. Both of us had learned, through painful experience, that the significant others in our lives were not receptive to the ideas and experiences we shared. Any attempt to discuss contact from 'beyond the veil' or metaphysical concepts met with derision or incomprehension. We found it best to keep such discussions between ourselves.

Asher and his mother, though, had opened my mind to spheres I'd barely dreamed of. I knew I had a great deal still to learn and Asher knew he still had much information to pass on to me.

I don't think the idea of putting it together in a book had occurred to either of us at that time, but I started to make copious notes of what he was telling me during our phone or email discussions and at the times when we were still able to meet for occasional days out.

With each passing year he became more certain and more able to explain what he knew, while I attempted to keep up by reading all I could find in the 'new science' and 'spirituality' sections of bookshops.

My reading amused and pleased Asher. I remember him following me around one of Cambridge's largest bookshops, asking what I was looking for.

"Something about time," I said.

"Good. That's relevant," he grinned. "What else?"

"Dimensions... maybe God..."

"Even more relevant," he nodded.

He showed no interest in reading the books himself, but listened carefully when I told him about their content. Sometimes the ideas would be new to him and he'd become very excited. More often, though, he would nod encouragingly, like an adult praising a small child's first faltering steps into literacy.

This was when I discovered another of his special talents — the one I mentioned in the opening chapter. I clearly remember an occasion when I was clutching my latest volume of metaphysics as we walked together through a town we were visiting. My progress through the book had been slow, as both the vocabulary and the ideas it contained were at the very limits of my understanding. I was attempting to paraphrase the parts I'd read for him and making a rather poor job of it.

"Just hold the book out flat, on the palm of your hand," Asher said impatiently.

I did so and he placed his own hand lightly on top of the book cover for a few moments. He then nodded, smiled and gave me a clear summary of all the major points — those I'd read and the ones I hadn't yet reached.

***

By this time, even *he* had become bored with the underground train journeys, so he acquired a collection of railway timetables and we planned longer excursions, usually travelling into London to change stations so that we could head off to other areas. Ours is a small country and we managed trips to hills and coastal towns in the south, the Norfolk Broads, the cities of the Midlands and even the mountains of Wales. Each journey, of course, gave us plenty of time to talk and it was while sitting in railway carriages that he shared some of his most fascinating 'knowing' with me.

One summer in his mid-teens, Ash began to experience premonitions. They clearly disturbed him and there were some he refused to share with me. Even those he did discuss were far from pleasant. He was clearly moved and upset by these visions, as if he could actually feel the suffering. He spoke of a chain of natural disasters, a much reduced world population and those people who were left becoming very different.

"I think I'll survive but I'm not sure you'll make it. I can't see you there," he sighed.

"But how can the future already be decided?" I wanted to know. "Doesn't that do away with free choice?"

He looked at me sadly and was silent for a long while.

Finally he replied, "There are infinite routes, but they all seem to lead to this one point."

Many years later, in one of our telepathic discussions, I asked him to expand on his claim that the people left after the world shift he had predicted would be 'different'. This was his reply:

A: To me it looks like there will be a grasp that there is a bigger picture — not just the idea of living life and having nothing else. It is making connections through the heart and mind so that we can all connect to the best way of living and putting that ahead of profit and wealth. Drinking in change that benefits the world.

Another prediction, made a few months later, was to do with some kind of major financial crash. Asher stared into the vision and become hugely frustrated that he didn't have the words to describe what he saw. He told me angrily that I didn't understand the full significance. He was right, of course, since all he'd been able to give me was the following, scribbled on a scrap of paper:

$$F(\ (p = n) > (p = B)\ )$$

If only we'd fully mastered telepathy and been able to use what came to be called our 'astral envelope' technique back then to convey information. How much easier it would have been for him simply to send me the concepts and visions he had as a thought package. Perhaps he was doing exactly that, but I had no way, back then, of receiving or interpreting it. I could often pick up on his raw emotions, even when we were in different locations, but not his thoughts, not the reasons behind those emotions and not the 'knowing' he laboured so hard to explain verbally. That ability would come much later, after many difficult years of separation.

Now, though, all that is possible, which is why I'm finally able to write this book. This year he was able to remember and telepathically explain the financial crash event.

A: Yes, I recall my frustration at not being able to explain that. It was about the repercussions of a financial collapse. I was seeing how it touched all aspects of society. I was trying to reach beyond the immediate chaotic aftermath into the change of mindset of the population en masse. It's actually very relevant to what we were discussing before.

J: You mean people needing a crisis for them to alter their mindset and embrace change?

A: Yes. The maths was my attempt to explain that, but it was pretty lame.

J: You were only fifteen. I thought it was quite inventive! So can you explain it this way or do you not recall it well enough?

A: I can recall it. I saw the financial collapse as the initiator of what followed. That's why the F is outside the brackets. The part inside the brackets shows a division within society. The first group has power from the new paradigm. They overcome or outnumber those who cling to the old materialist patterns of existing. Those people — the second lot — scrabble around for possessions/objects. The others — the 'n' ones — become more focused on co-operating and rebuilding a sustainable life and structure.

J: So clearly this change has yet to happen. Do you see the 'routes' you spoke of converging more closely towards it?

A: Yes, I believe it will come. I'm not sure how it comes about.

At that point in our telepathic discussion I received the word 'china' and wondered whether Asher was telling me that China would be involved in causing the change. I felt him laughing as he assured me that was *not* the message he'd intended to send.

Perhaps I need to expand a little on how our dialogues work. Asher uses pure thought to communicate. He sends ideas, concepts and intentions to me and, in ways that I don't fully understand, my mind transforms them into words. The actual words, therefore, are usually mine because that's the way I make sense of thoughts. As I write down my replies to him, I also 'think' them, of course, and it is the thoughts that he picks up. Usually it works very smoothly but on this occasion there was some confusion.

Asher explained that the reference to 'china' was not to the country, but to a vision I'd received a few days earlier and discussed with him. I had seen each human as a ceramic vessel, with the 'cracked vessels' — the people labelled by experts as disordered or dysfunctional in some way — having a brilliant light shining through those cracks. It was this thought he had tried to convey to me when I misunderstood the 'china' reference.

A: It was an image of cracked china vessels, like the ones you spoke about, breaking apart to let the light show. There would be access to all the knowledge/'knowing' for those who had opened to it by then. The rest would be so busy trying to keep their vessels intact, they would see nothing.

J: So what would happen to them?

A: Remember when lockdown came at the start of the coronavirus outbreak and the rich couldn't function without the servants and nannies? It would be like that.

J: So only those who can be self-sufficient will survive?

A: Exactly that, yes.

J: Do you feel the process has started or is imminent, or don't you have a timeframe?

A: The timing will depend on the speed of the changes taking place now but it's not decided as yet.

***

I hope this chapter has given you some insight into the levels of 'knowing' Asher had access to during his adolescence. I found the information he gave me fascinating at the time, but even more so now that I can pick up on the detailed explanations he is able to give me.

There was one week, though, which stood out from the rest and was astonishing, even by his standards. That week deserves a chapter of its own.

Chapter 9

The Map, the Bottle and a Buffet Queue

The esoteric and the prosaic travelled companionably side by side on our journeys around the time the events in this chapter took place. It had been almost ten years since Asher had first exploded into my life. He was now a gangly six-foot adolescent while I was a portly middle-aged schoolmistress, so we must have presented a strange picture to anyone observing us.

One minute he was the teacher, the next it was me; for while he eagerly used his ever-developing language skills to guide me through the dimensions he could see and I could only dream of, I remained true to the promise I had made to his mother and continued to help him develop the social skills and confidence he would need to manage an independent life on Planet Earth.

I'd become used to the sudden revelations which seemed to arrive in his mind from outside of time and ordinary human experience. Did I suspect that he knew far more than he was letting on? Definitely. I'd learned, though, that more would be revealed if I waited patiently and listened very carefully.

Ah, but how would you feel if someone told you they had a map of all the atoms in the universe?

Asher was fifteen when he made that announcement. Even from him, it sounded a fairly extravagant claim. I had no idea how to respond to it and he sensed my slight scepticism.

"I can make you a copy of it if you want," he offered. "It's in my mind. I *know* it."

There was always a slightly hopeful smile as he shared his truths with me; a look that said something like, 'I don't know whether or not you're ready for this, but let's give it a try.'

***

Several years before, I'd commented to him that he was the most 'open' kid I'd ever met. "Is there anything you *don't* believe in?" I had asked.

He'd thought for a moment then said, "No, I don't think there is. It's less complicated this way."

I'd decided he had a point, so on this occasion I told him that yes, I would very much like a copy of this map of his and he promised to bring it with him on our next train journey.

The following Saturday, after we'd bought our tickets to a remote village in the heart of the South Downs and settled into our seats on the first train, he presented me with a sheet of A4 paper. I examined it. I'm not sure what I'd been expecting, but not this.

It had been printed out from his computer — a neat grid of identical circles covering the page. No other features, no key, no words, just circles stretching as far as the page would allow. I looked at him quizzically. Perhaps this was the only time I wondered whether all the revelations and predictions were some sort of elaborate trick he played on me.

Asher read my mind — of course he did.

"It's the only way I could think of to show it to you," he said. "The movement of a single molecule will affect something light years away."

I shook my head sadly. I had no idea what he was talking about and at that time Asher was unable to access sufficient words to explain further, leaving both of us feeling frustrated at the gulf between our respective levels of understanding.

***

Once again (*that's the joy of writing a book: we can travel through time*), I will move forward fifteen years and ask the adult Asher, now freed from the limitations of spoken language and able to share his ideas lucidly via telepathic thought, if he can help me understand the map.

A: It's really quite simple. Do you remember the diagram I gave you?

J: Yes. I still have it somewhere. A grid of circles touching but not overlapping. Very symmetrical, all in rows and columns.

A: That's right. See it at any scale you like. It can be atoms or people or galaxies.

J: Right, I understand that, but in what way is it a map?

A: A design that allows each unit to hold a space, but it can only maintain its position/sovereignty/structure when supported by the grid. So the strength is in both the overall configuration and the individual integrity of the single unit. We are at once independent of and utterly dependent on the rest, supporting each other and being supported in equal measure. The way every part builds on and supports and is held up by the rest of the structure means no one part is more important than another.

J: What a cosmos!

A: Yes.

***

Returning now to that train journey, as we sped towards London for our transfer, Asher was thinking quietly, pondering on how he could help me to better understand the workings of the universe.

We were sitting opposite one another in the carriage. He had a plastic bottle of water on his side of the table that lay between us. His eyes fell on it and suddenly he had an idea.

"See this water bottle? How could you move it across the table without touching it?" he asked.

I peered at the bottle. It was almost full, so too heavy to blow. The table was bolted to the carriage floor, so there was no way of moving that. I suspected that Asher was looking for a more cryptic solution.

"Is it something to do with those molecules you were talking about? Using the power of thought to take them from in front of the bottle and placing them behind it in some way?"

Ash gave a snort of impatience. "That's such a long way round! It's far easier than that. *See* it where you want it to be!"

Obediently, I let my gaze settle on my side of the table. I did my best to imagine the bottle in its new position, but my whole life experience up to that point told me that bottles of water did not spontaneously migrate across tables. I looked at Asher, but he had a confident smile and was watching the table carefully.

About five minutes later the door at the end of our carriage slid open and the train guard came through to check everyone's tickets. This was standard procedure.

"Tickets please," he said, as he approached us. He took my ticket from me, looked at it, smiled, clipped it and handed it back. The same procedure followed as he checked Ash's ticket. At some point during that short process, for absolutely no discernible reason, the guard picked up the water bottle and moved it across the table so that it was in front of me, before continuing on to the next group of passengers.

I stared in total disbelief, while Asher gave me a calm but mildly triumphant grin.

Perhaps I asked more questions and probably he gave me more enigmatic answers that day, but I didn't write them down and can no longer remember them. Certainly I must have badgered him for an explanation that I could understand, because a few days later he rather grandly announced that he had decided to tell me a *little* more about how it worked. He was at great pains to explain that he was giving me only *some* of the information he was aware of. That time I did write his words down, so here they are:

"With energy transferring, like moving that bottle, it works much more easily if you work with things that are more likely to happen, so you're just altering them maybe a bit, in ways they'd be likely to change, rather than trying to do something very unlikely. Then you'd be working against a bigger force. That's not impossible, but it's a lot more effort."

Even now, all these years later, I still sense a high level of exasperation in Asher at my difficulty in understanding what happened that day. His 'telepathic self' is, though, much more able and willing to explain the process than he was as a teenage boy, half a lifetime ago.

Here is some information he gave me recently:

J: Suppose we go back to the bottle of water in the train carriage. I saw it move. I saw how it moved but I don't understand the process.

A: OK. It has to do with focus and intention. I set in my mind the idea that the bottle needed to move across to the other side. I moved my awareness forward to the point at which the bottle was there. Is that clear?

J: Hmm, kind of. The bottle is at point A. You need the bottle to be at point B. So is it a case of imagining it there, or is there more to it than that?

A: It's more than imagining, yes. Imagination is powerful in a general sense, but this is intention. You control your world. It doesn't exist outside of your perception.

J: But I was there, you were there and we both saw that guy move it. So whose perception was that? It seems to have been yours, mine and his.

A: I told you to see the bottle on the other side of the table. You and I were both doing that. We saw it as being able to move to point B, agreed?

J: Yes...

A: So that was the process. The intervening part was just filled in, in a way that made sense to our physical senses in this reality. It could have been a gust of wind, someone staggering as they passed our table and knocking it or the guard moving it aside. The 'how' doesn't matter.

J: Did you influence the guard to move it?

A: The guard doesn't matter. If the bottle had simply teleported, that wouldn't have been consistent with our form of reality.

J: You avoided my question.

A: It's like playing chess. When you see an opening, you use it to your advantage.

J: So you did! You saw the guard come into the carriage to check our tickets and you influenced him somehow to move the bottle, yes?

A: Or maybe you did...

J: So you do it by brainwashing people?

A: No! It really isn't like that. It isn't the way it happens that matters. You have situation A. You intend situation B. You then wait for life to join up the dots between the two.

J: I've spent hours staring at candle flames, trying to influence which way they move. Can't do it.

A: You've spent hours thinking how such things can't happen. It's time to stop doing that and to see the result you want. Then wait for the events to fall into place.

J: I'm sort of getting what you're saying and I agree that conviction would help a lot. Any other hints?

A: Focus and intention and letting life join up the dots. You're far more powerful than you think.

***

Our day in the South Downs continued in an oddly normal way. Asher was cheerfully poking around the railway yard, enjoying the mechanical exhibits in the small museum and laughing and chattering as we strolled along the river bank in the warm autumn sunshine. I was doing my best to join in, whilst trying once again to adjust my view of how life works.

On the journey home we were both pleasantly tired, but hungry and thirsty. As I mentioned earlier, while Asher was busily instructing me in the workings of the cosmos, I was still finding ways to boost his confidence when coping with ordinary day-to-day activities. His adolescent awkwardness and autistic spectrum perception combined to make him quite shy about coping with everyday responsibilities and I was helping him with this, setting him small, achievable tasks that would raise his self-esteem.

"There's a buffet car two carriages down," I told him. "Why don't you go and buy us both a drink and something to eat?"

He craned his neck to see through the train. "Queue's too long," he announced. "I will do it, but I need to get rid of the queue first."

I watched curiously as the familiar slight smile returned to his face and he stared for a while into the middle distance.

Eventually he grinned at me and asked what I wanted from the buffet. It would be fine for him to go there now, he said, as there was no queue. I noted that he hadn't turned round to look and check whether this was the case. With a jubilant smile, he stood up, headed through the carriage and was back, just moments later, from the now empty buffet car, balancing our drinks and two toasted sandwiches.

"You didn't say what sort you wanted, but I know you like mushrooms, so I got you cheese and mushroom. That OK?"

I assured him it was perfect and congratulated him on a task achieved.

"But the queue?" I asked. "Did you influence that in some way, like the bottle this morning?"

"Mmm," he nodded, as he chomped on his snack. "Same sort of thing really."

I suspect that for Asher, buying the food and drink had been far more of a challenge than mysteriously removing the bustling queue of hungry passengers.

Chapter 10

Mountains to Climb

Ash had loved hills and mountains all his life. He always seemed at his happiest and most relaxed when clambering to the top of a hill and standing triumphantly on the summit, while I puffed along behind.

Recently, I asked him why they were so special to him.

J: Can you tell me why you've always had this deep love for hills and mountains?

A: There's something symbolic about climbing a hill, like a pilgrimage or rite of passage. The energy is lighter — less stuck — at the top of a hill or mountain. I feel freer.

***

We never climbed further than the foothills of an actual mountain, but there were many metaphorical peaks to conquer as he moved towards adulthood.

Receiving, in his teens, an official diagnosis of Asperger's Syndrome, as his type of autistic perception was then labelled, hit him hard. He had always been aware of the differences between himself and most of his classmates in the mainstream secondary school he attended and the need to lead a double life in terms of how he behaved and what he revealed to them, but while he had previously (and with encouragement from me) seen his differences as a kind of extra bonus to his everyday life, being told by a doctor all that was 'wrong' with him compared to 'normal' people had an unsurprisingly negative effect. That fragile self-confidence took a nosedive and he began to shut himself away alone for long periods of time.

Our outings became fewer and further between and what he had once viewed as his unusual but valuable ability to see into realms most humans failed to recognise now struck him as yet another sign of oddness, and therefore a symptom of his disability.

I made every effort to persuade him otherwise, but mine was a lone voice against the might of the medical establishment and the endless articles about this supposed pathology he read on the internet. He, he told me in his darkest moments, was mentally disabled and if I thought any different and believed all the things he'd told me in the past, I was delusional.

On very rare occasions I coaxed him into the outside world, found tempting places to visit and tried to resume our metaphysical discussions and thus his self-belief.

On one such day we had forced our way through blustery weather and made slow progress up a steep slope in the Surrey Downs. Asher was subdued and we trudged in silence for a while, the wind whipping into us on the exposed hilltop. Eventually, he spoke.

"I've found a way of getting to this other place," he told me. "But don't ask me to describe it, because there are no words."

As I considered this unexpected revelation, he glanced anxiously at me. "Don't want to answer any more questions, OK?"

I shrugged and we moved along the path, gradually descending into a more sheltered combe. We turned a corner and there before us, set in beautiful but overgrown parkland, with high metal fences and gates rusty and padlocked, stood a huge, deserted building, with a faded sign proclaiming it to be a 'lunatic asylum' — a shocking and tragic remnant of the previous century.

We both stared wordlessly, thinking our own thoughts until, in a brief moment of candour, he turned to me with an agonised expression on his face.

"Look," he said, "I'm just too lazy to do it. I know what I'm supposed to do. I know why I chose this life and what my plan was, but I'm too lazy. It's so much easier to just ignore all that stuff and get on with trying to live like other people. That's hard enough!"

Unlike Asher, I *didn't* know what his life plan held. I guessed it was something special, but all I could see beside me was a tortured boy on the edge of adulthood who had had the rug pulled away from under him in more ways than one. As well as the shock of the Asperger's diagnosis, he had the stresses of end-of-school exams to cope with and the uncertainty of what life would hold after that.

I nodded sadly, assured him that I'd always be there to lend help and support, but acknowledged that if he needed a break from our discussions and to be left to make his own choices, I would respect that and step back.

We carried on along the path towards the railway station. Asher seemed calmer now. Once there, we found there would be a long while to wait for the next train on this tiny branch line. I unpacked the food I'd brought with me and we sat on a bench on the platform to eat it, while we chattered about everyday subjects.

Asher's mood, though, had changed again. It was dizzying to try to keep up with him at times.

"I could teach you to do it, that travelling thing, if you want? Then you could do it yourself and I wouldn't have to explain it all to you."

"OK," I agreed. "I'm happy to give it a try."

***

Now he was in full tutor mode.

"Sit up straight and stare straight ahead of you," he instructed.

I looked across the track to the opposite platform and the scrubby trees and bushes beyond.

"Now let your eyes go kind of blurry," he told me.

I smiled, imagining a meditation instructor telling me to 'soften my gaze' and did so.

"Right, now you need to act like you're going to sleep but don't actually fall asleep and keep your eyes sort of shut halfway. Stay like that for about ten or fifteen minutes, then you'll start to see amazing things."

I did my best. I really did. I was vaguely aware that Asher was watching me carefully but I tried to allow my mind to empty. Suddenly there was a deep sigh from beside me.

"It's no good," Ash told me sadly. "You won't be able to do it. I've looked in your mind and you're not ready."

The disappointment on his face and in his voice was very evident. This had been his last hope: to hand over the mantle to me and leave me to work my way through the hidden realms which he believed it had been his destiny to explore.

He was walking between two worlds. The new discoveries in the secret realms intrigued and drew him to investigate further, but the pressures of his daily life had become so intense and heavy that he was afraid to do so.

I wished I could take some of the weight from his young shoulders, but the best I could do for the time being was what I'd promised on the hill, to pull back temporarily and allow him to deal with the parts of his life we didn't share.

***

More recently, I asked him telepathically to talk me through his mindset as it was at that time:

J: What were your feelings about your psychic abilities and knowledge during your teenage years?

A: I had a lot of mood swings. I was finding it very hard to cope with school. I wanted to fit in and be like everyone else, but it was difficult. Sometimes I just didn't have the energy or willpower to think about all the psychic material. It was like an extra layer of clothing that was weighing me down and making me feel uncomfortable. There were times I just wanted to take it off and focus on ordinary life.

J: Yes, I can see exactly what you mean. Fitting in with others is so important at that age. But you didn't abandon it completely.

A: No, I didn't. The trouble was, normal things that interested my classmates, like football and motorbikes, didn't grab me at all. It was a strain to pretend to be interested in them. I was far more inclined to watch sci-fi films and then I would start to think about them and see the parts that set me off thinking about the things I 'knew' or could discover if I focused on them.

J: And you didn't find any school friends who shared your interests or had similar skills?

A: No. I started to be quite solitary except when I saw you and we went on our journeys. I had a lot of anxiety attacks and one of the things I was scared of was someone from school seeing me at the station or somewhere with you, because they would have bullied me about that.

J: Yes, I can see what a difficult time that was for you. In fact, I got quite a bit of stick from family and friends for hanging around with a teenage boy! We didn't plan that part of our 'contract' very well, did we — the age difference?

A: No, it was quite awkward. When I was sixteen I went for several months without having any contact with you.

***

There followed, then, those months of silence between us. Asher sent me his exam results and we briefly discussed them, but then the shutters came down again and I was left wondering, hoping and pursuing some investigations of my own.

Chapter 11

Channel

I sometimes wonder how different our lives might have been if I had decided not to take that teaching job in the specialist unit, or if Asher's parents had chosen to leave him in a mainstream school rather than sending him there. I suppose Asher would say that we *had* to meet, because all the possibilities pointed to that moment in time.

There are aspects of my life, of course, that would barely have been any different; I'd still have taught classes, parented my children and met up with friends. I didn't share Asher's teachings with any of them, so they would have seen no difference. This secret life, conducted largely in railway carriages and logged in various well-concealed notebooks, would have been missing, though. And what a loss that would have been for me. The vague and unfulfilled curiosity which had niggled away in my mind since my earliest years was being, during my time with Asher, satisfied and expanded in equal measure. He knew nothing of educational philosophy, yet his 'Socratic method' of teaching — asking just the right question to enable the learner to reach deep levels of understanding — was faultless. Without his intervention, I would never have attained my current level of engagement with life's mysteries which has been and continues to be so inspiring and revelatory as each day passes.

As for Ash, would he have shared his 'knowing' with someone else if he hadn't found me? I was the only person he spoke to about such matters. Perhaps there was some back-up figure, waiting in the wings to take my place if I failed to show up... or perhaps he'd have carried on wondering in silence.

I'm very glad we met.

I can't pretend that the withdrawal wasn't difficult for me. Ash had been a huge part of my life for many years and I'd enjoyed his company and revelations for all of that time. Of course I recognised that, apart from anything else, he was of an age when spending time with his old primary school teacher was not hugely appealing. I had, after all, raised three children of my own and watched as, one by one, they had flown the nest.

It was during that silent summer, when I was occupying myself by continuing my own research into all things metaphysical, that I came upon a blog written by a couple who lived overseas. I'll call them John and Sarah.

Sarah was a channel for a group of non-physical elders. She spoke their words while John carefully recorded the wisdom the guides shared and posted it in a blog. They generously encouraged blog readers to send in questions which John then put to the elders, as they spoke through his wife, and published in his posts.

By this time I was very familiar with the writings of White Eagle, the Conversations with God of Neale Donald Walsch and the Seth Material channelled by Jane Roberts and recorded by her husband Robert Butts. I read through pages and pages of John and Sarah's writing and recognised the quality and authenticity of the wisdom that came through.

For so long now, I had kept my conversations with Asher largely to myself, having no idea who to share them with. Finally I felt I had found someone who could, perhaps, help me to make some sense of it all.

With more than a little trepidation, I wrote Sarah and John a message, briefly outlining the history I shared with Ash, and asking if their guides could offer any explanation for this highly unconventional friendship and whether or not it had now run its course.

This was just the beginning of a long and fascinating dialogue with these delightful people and their guides. The information

I received was sometimes shocking, sometimes challenging and sometimes comforting. At last I had found someone who not only understood but offered guidance and advice.

There was a great deal of information, over the following months and years, but I will try to summarise the main points here.

Asher and I had indeed, the elders told me through Sarah, planned to incarnate into this lifetime and to meet up. We had, apparently, had many other lifetimes together, taking on various roles in relation to one another. They wished to draw my attention to one in Atlantis, in which we had again chosen to be teacher and pupil. He had been an extremely gifted student and had gone on to assist me in my classroom as we taught very small children how to use telepathy. They said that we had chosen to repeat those roles in the current lifetime and that once again, we had decided to work with telepathic communication.

This revelation came many years before Asher and I managed to establish our current level of communication, but of course I recalled the incidents back in the speech and language classes and the many times since when I had been able to pick up his emotions, even from many miles away, or the numerous occasions when he had apparently read my mind.

The elders insisted that I should mentally send him my good wishes, even at times when he was not being responsive, and then wait patiently and quietly, trusting any replies that came into my mind. Obviously, I was more than happy to send good wishes to Asher mentally, but it was to be at least another ten years before I managed to trust my mind sufficiently to expect or receive any responses from him. Nevertheless, the seed had been sown and I was excited at the possibility.

The other message they had for me at that time was that I needed to write our story in a book and publish it, so that others could learn from our experiences. I was urged to make this a priority in my life as what we were doing and about to do would be inspiring and uplifting.

"This book must be written," they insisted.

That instruction, when I relayed it to Asher, was met with a stony refusal. "I forbid you to write my life story," he told me, flatly.

I put the project aside, but every so often a few notes were quietly added to the file I was keeping on my computer. I hoped that at some point in the future he might relent, which is, of course, what happened.

***

By the time Asher reached his late teens, our lives had moved on. He had finished school, turned his back on education, relocated to London and was in a steady job. My life had changed too. My children had grown up and I moved much further away, to a place where people who shared my interests in spirituality and metaphysics congregated. Like Asher, I'd become disillusioned with the education system and worked instead on building up an alternative educational environment: a meeting, socialising and learning club for home-educated children, many of whom had a diagnosis of autistic spectrum perception, ADHD or otherwise struggled to fit in with school life. This is where I worked for the next part of my life.

Asher and I remained in contact, but it veered wildly between times when there were frequent phone chats, long emails and occasional meetings in some place we could both reach, to weeks or even months at a time when he kept very much to himself and restricted his messages to a word or two a week, just to let me know he was 'fine'.

My conversations with John, Sarah and the elders encouraged me to start discussing some of the experiences Asher and I had shared with a few other people.

In my new town, I was able to meet some psychically gifted people and to get to know a few like-minded friends. I'll always be grateful to those who listened and took an interest in our story, accepting that Asher was indeed a remarkable young man with stunning abilities. He too, in his more receptive moments, was pleased and grateful that others took an interest in the things he had told me and were able to recognise the wisdom in them.

Part III

Asher Exploring

Chapter 12

Tools of the Trade

As Asher settled into life as a young adult, coping with the everyday challenges of managing his autistic perception in a predominantly neurotypical society as well as living and working in a huge, bustling city, it is very much to his credit that he continued to work with his unusual abilities and the 'knowing' he was continuing to acquire. In this chapter I will outline what I know (or have since been able to discover) about his psi activities.

***

Ash had formed a special affinity with crystals ever since I first bought him an aventurine stone when he was a young child.

I recall him standing in the shop exclaiming, "Whoa! I can feel it pulsing. Are they meant to do that?"

By the time in which this chapter is set he had amassed quite a collection.

***

Once we started (some twelve years later) communicating regularly via telepathy, he suggested that I should hold a quartz crystal to boost the signal if I was having difficulty picking up his thoughts, pointing out that quartz is used extensively in modern communication technology. I took the opportunity to ask him how he had used crystals during his 'exploring' phase.

A: I treated crystals with great respect. They concentrated Light for me. By holding and focusing on a crystal, I could enhance my ability to travel beyond the physical. They also worked as transmitters. I used them to amplify my intentions.

J: Interesting. Could you give me an example of how you used them in that way?

A: I would place them in various patterns, very much by trial and error, and discern ways to manipulate material situations, mostly protecting my possessions and remaining safe.

I should add that at this time in his life, having had a very frightening encounter with a mugger in a local street, as well as having money stolen from his room in the house he shared, Asher felt under pressure to use all means possible to protect himself, his phone and his computer.

***

While he was in his late teens, he also discovered and became fascinated by dowsing rods, quickly mastering ways to use them that extended far beyond seeking out watercourses. He took to writing and sending me articles about what he called Ancient Technology. These were fascinating and carefully written. However, as his exploration of the hidden realms developed and extended, the material he sent became more esoteric and mysterious. It was also often laced with somewhat extravagant claims. The following extract is a typical example:

***

An experienced and sufficiently enlightened user could use a pair of dowsing rods to achieve anything one desires. The rods can harness power from crystals and leys as well as any other energy source including pure psychic energy. The rods can alter the sub-atomic structure of the universe. They can provide interaction with different dimensions. They can provide the user with unlimited knowledge.

***

That was quite a statement. I tried in vain to get him to explain and expand on the information he was sharing, or to answer my many questions about it. He wasn't prepared to do so at that point in his life. He insisted that the articles were all he was willing to divulge and I would have to be content with that.

Fortunately, we have moved a long way since then, and recently I asked him telepathically to explain what he was discovering back then.

J: You made many claims about dowsing rods, although I don't think I ever saw you using them. Can you explain what you meant?

A: I was amazed and delighted by the power I discovered in these simple tools. Up until then, I simply 'knew' things, but when I was able to master the rods, I realised they worked not just to find underground water or to track leys (energy lines on the planet's surface) *but could pick up fluctuations in psychological, non-physical realms. It was a new experience for me to be able to see actual 3D objects interacting with aspects of the cosmos I'd assumed were not detectable by physical means.*

J: Yes, I can imagine the effect that would have had on you. I felt much the same when I found I could use a pendulum to communicate with your mother.

A: Exactly. Opening up, quite literally, a new world.

J: You made the point that a user would need to be 'experienced and sufficiently enlightened' but said they could achieve anything they desired, including altering 'the sub-atomic structure of the universe'. Can you comment on that?

A: I was referring to interdimensional dowsing. There are certain tools and technologies, largely forgotten in modern times, that can be used by someone with enough intuition to find the places where the boundaries between domains are thin or warped in some way. I realised that meant one could either locate such a 'portal' or use the glitch in the membrane to create one.

J: Would that be by dowsing over a map or in the actual location?

A: Either is possible but the boundaries (that's not the right word, but there isn't a better one) fluctuate as the physical world and the non-physical realm are constantly in formation, because of the changes created by the consciousness of sentient beings.

J: So are you saying that we not only change our world physically (by digging, planting, building, destroying and so on) but we also affect the membrane/borders between the physical and metaphysical realms?

A: Yes. It's in a constant state of flux by its very nature. Plants and trees affect it in both directions, just as humans and animals do. My point was that the sensitive use of tools like crystals and dowsing rods can manipulate the boundaries to a greater degree than mere life processes and choices.

It's like the air around us being subtly changed all the time by people inhaling and exhaling, but if someone brought in an electric air blower of some sort, the air quality and temperature would change abruptly in that area.

***

My own baseline level knowledge of science was embarrassingly low, having had an education focused on literature and the arts. I'd not been particularly impressed by the fundamentalist mainstream science I had to teach at primary school as part of the National Curriculum. A great deal about it had instinctively felt wrong, or at least incomplete. However, in an attempt to keep pace with Asher's ideas and their implications for the way the world *really* works, I have given over a great deal of time and effort to listen to lectures and read all that I can. In so doing, I've discovered that there is much current research in quantum physics and cosmology which supports his claims about the nature of consciousness and the links between what theoretical physicist David Bohm called the Implicate and Explicate Orders

— the physical and non-physical realms — in-forming each other and constantly changing and expanding.

Much as I would have enjoyed observing Asher working with his dowsing rods, pendulum and crystals, he needed at this point in his life to be free to explore by himself. In another of his articles, he explained:

***

Every person is born with a different level of psychic ability. Though for some it may be too low to notice, for others it is an amazing ability with limitless potential.

With every generation a higher percentage of the human race is born with higher levels. It is possible to increase someone's levels through psychic activities, including using crystals, dowsing rods and other similar items. Expanding someone's knowledge of psychic phenomena and related issues also assists in raising their level.

***

It was interesting to receive these occasional articles from Asher via email, but living at opposite sides of the country as we now did, I found myself wanting to engage in more direct research with him. Fortunately, once I had formed that intention, life served to 'join up the dots', as Ash had once put it and I was given the opportunity to do exactly that, but without the need for any lengthy train journeys!

Chapter 13

Working Remotely

When Ash had reached his mid-twenties and I had more or less retired from education, an interesting synchronicity took our secret life in a new direction.

I strongly suspect that my subtle-light navigation system was once more in action when I decided one day to watch a video about remote viewing. I had heard of this technique without ever taking much notice before, but once I understood it, I immediately felt this was something that would be of interest to Asher. I messaged him to explain the basic principles and suggested it might be fun to try. As I had expected, he was very keen to explore this new way of working.

For those not familiar with RV, it involves a person attempting to mentally view a target of some kind from a remote location and to record the impressions they receive by drawing or writing notes.

To begin with, we set the bar fairly low. We would select a time at the weekend for one of us to hold a crystal and focus on it for ten minutes or so, while the other worked to pick up any features of the stone. To our delight, we found we could both get good results. The colour, an idea of the shape and size, whether it was translucent or opaque and any particular features would somehow come into the mind of the person attempting to view the stone remotely. We would then exchange photographs and jottings to determine how successful we were.

Ash proved to be particularly adept at this way of working. Here he explains how the process of remote viewing is experienced from the viewer's perspective:

***

When I say 'see' it's more of a visualising of the feelings that I get, which I suspect is highly influenced by my logical mind trying to form a likely interpretation of the feelings, than say a vision or anything that compares with how I ordinarily see using my eyes.

***

As he became more proficient and used to working in this way, he also wrote about the altered state needed to engage successfully in remote viewing:

***

It is necessary to be able to correctly focus at the correct time, while ensuring that the knowledge held is sufficiently minimalistic to avoid involuntary logical assumptions from clouding the receipt of information through remote viewing, but sufficient to ensure the information received can be interpreted correctly.

***

I am struck by how very similar this way of being is to that defined in 1817 by the poet John Keats as 'negative capability': *"being in uncertainties, mysteries, doubts, without any irritable reaching after fact and reason"*.

As you can no doubt imagine, our exploration of remote viewing rapidly moved on from staring at crystals to more ambitious and varied targets. Here's an account of some of our RV adventures, which I wrote at the time we were doing them regularly:

***

It's Sunday afternoon and I'm standing in a garden centre, sheltering from a heavy spring shower in one of the polytunnels. Outside are flowerbeds, benches covered in pot plants and windbreaks supporting tubs of trees. I text Asher to tell him I'm in position and ready to begin. He texts back, "Start now" and I spend the next ten minutes looking carefully at everything around me, drinking in the sights, sounds, scents and textures of the place.

He's moved on from viewing a crystal held in my hand to viewing locations. He has no clue as to where I am. He's sitting in a room across the country and simply knows that I have chosen a venue and will remain there for ten minutes. He focuses on me and tries, with some sense way beyond the physical, to pick up impressions of the place I'm in.

Time's up. I take photos. He, meanwhile, is drawing and annotating a sketch of what he 'saw'. I receive a message:

"Hope you can make this picture out and my handwriting. Also think water might be involved somewhere."

I look skywards and grin. Plenty of wet stuff. Then I look at his drawing. He's viewed it from several yards away from where I was standing. The flowers are there. He's drawn one of the benches, presumably the one covered in concrete planting pots, and one of the tree-support windbreaks, which he's labelled "Structure, free-standing". Three items he's annotated as 'hills' drawn in the background are in the right position for the three polytunnels. They have green coverings — very hill-like.

"It's good," I tell him, and send some of the photos I've taken.

***

Every weekend there are new wonders: he drew a medieval barn I passed on the way to a site. I'd paused long enough to consider using it but discounted it as it was closed to the public and would be far better on a day when I could stand inside. How, then, did he draw an *interior* view of it, with the roof trusses that couldn't be seen from the outside?

***

Distant viewing, X-ray viewing and, as next become apparent, future viewing.

On a couple of occasions, he'd managed to pick up details of one of my crystals before I had focused on it. He pointed out, though, that he knew in those cases what he was trying to home in on. With a location viewing, he had no idea where to hunt. All he knew was that he was searching for wherever I would be on the Sunday at a set time.

One Saturday he did just that. He made some notes in advance of what he 'saw' and waited for the Sunday session. My son was visiting me. I'd explained this odd activity Asher and I engaged in to him and he shrugged and agreed to come and watch. It was he who suggested the location — and not until Sunday morning.

The day before it had even been chosen, then, Asher had correctly identified the tower of a church and claimed there was something round on the ground nearby. We searched the floor of the church for a match but I was unable to identify the round object he had viewed. It had to be there somewhere. Finally it was my son who solved that one.

"Ash must have seen the circular labyrinth laid out in the church grounds," he said.

I headed back to take a photo and sent it to Asher. It was a match.

***

Even to Asher, with his extensive 'knowing' and awareness of what remains hidden from many of us, this ability to view an event that had not yet occurred was intriguing. We decided to test it further.

On one occasion I'd asked him if he could view my location at a specific time, six days ahead of the date when the event took place. I already knew where I would be, having a planned appointment, so it was a good chance for us to test out his viewing skills ahead of time. Sure enough, he came up with several very specific features of the room I'd be in and the surrounding area.

Buoyed up by our success, we tried a second viewing the next week, in which, again, I was quite certain where I would be and, once more, he nailed it. Obviously we were delighted with this proof that remote viewing seemed to work equally well for present and future events. Nevertheless, it raised some interesting questions.

What if I had changed my mind in the intervening days and decided not to go where I had originally planned to be? What if some misadventure had befallen me on my journey, preventing me from reaching my destination? Was he viewing my *intention*, rather than my future reality? Conversely, was it perhaps some kind of quantum weirdness? Was he, in effect, peering into the box where Schrodinger's unfortunate cat was suspended between possible outcomes and, by becoming the observer, collapsing the wave of probability and determining which would play out? In short, once he had done the viewing, was my future then set in stone? Clearly it wasn't. Obviously there would not be some supernatural force propelling me to the location he had viewed me in if I decided to stay in bed that morning. I still had free choice. In which case, how was his viewing so accurate, given that the event was yet to take place? We thought long and hard about all the ramifications and Asher finally concluded that remote viewing must be connected to probability. He felt that what he was seeing was the *most probable* place I would be on the target date and time.

***

I had been mulling over these ideas in my mind, wondering how we could refine our understanding of the processes involved. Synchronicity struck again, providing us with the perfect test for his theory. Here's what happened:

I had arranged to travel across the country to meet someone at a specific time and destination. My journey involved two train rides, with a change at the massive Birmingham New Street Station during rush hour. Because of that, I'd factored in a 25-minute transfer time at New Street. However, there I was, on my first train, finding that it was running 20 minutes late and my transfer time was shrinking rapidly.

The odds of making my connection seemed to be about 50:50. My current train might or might not make up some time on the journey. I might or might not locate and reach my next platform quickly when I arrived in Birmingham. There might or might not be delays caused by crowding on the escalators. My second train might or might not also be delayed.

Instinctively, I messaged Ash and told him I was unsure as to whether or not I would make a train connection and asked if he could view where I would be at 6:40 that evening, a short while after my final train was due to arrive. I reasoned that if he saw me at my destination, I could relax, knowing I'd make it. If he saw me on a train, though, I'd know it was likely I would miss my connection and be on a later one. A few minutes later, he got back to me. His viewing was unlike any we had experienced. He saw 'a long narrow dark area with rows of things along the sides'. There were no colours or identifying features, and we were both unsure what it meant.

As it turned out, I did make the rail connection, so that by 6:40 I was in my host's home. It had two adjoining rooms, with a narrow passageway through them and items of furniture to each side. But one could argue that a train carriage is laid out in the same way. The light had been switched on when we got into his home, so the house wasn't dark, but nor would a train carriage be. Curious.

A day or two later, I was on another rail journey. I decided to run a check, by asking Ash if he could view where I was. This time his response was that I was on a train. He saw it travelling through mountains and even told me the colour of the seats and the train's livery. All correct. He was clearly still an expert at this. So why the mysterious dark space in the other viewing?

To me it seems Asher's idea that *probability* is involved has been vindicated. I had asked him to view a future that was hanging in the balance. The outcome depended on several factors, all beyond my control, and there was a more or less equal chance that I would/would not catch the second train. In that circumstance, it seems, Asher was unable to pick up a clear indication of where I would be. The long dark area could represent an uncertain future. The items at the sides might be the two possibilities ranged along it. The more I have considered the situation, though — and Asher tells me telepathically that he believes this to be the correct interpretation — it appears that what he was seeing was in fact *both* possible scenarios at once, superimposed on each other and thus darkening and obscuring his view.

Chapter 14

The Energies Thing

There was plenty to be discovered, for both Asher and me, through our forays into remote viewing. One thing we hadn't worked out, though, was the inconsistency of the results. Sometimes the degree of accuracy was astonishing but on other, apparently similar, location viewings they were less impressive. Sometimes he would find features I couldn't identify. At others he would miss what I would imagine to be the main or obvious aspects of a site. Although there were always some matches and links, enough to assure us that a connection was being formed and information was transferring between us, the variability concerned him.

On one particular viewing, for example, there seemed to be fewer matches than usual. I'd chosen what seemed to me to be an excellent location: an ancient chapel and row of almshouses set in beautifully tended gardens. He found one or two small details but nothing that positively identified the place. As I thought we'd finished, a final text came through.

"I tried to do an advance viewing of this yesterday. Here's what I came up with. Does any of this mean anything to you?"

He'd attached a sheet with a few jottings. In large print were the words:

"Light? Fire?"

Immediately I realised what had happened. When I had entered the chapel to prepare for Ash's viewing, I'd had a sudden impulse to light a candle for my mother (who had passed over exactly two years before) and place it in the bowl in front of the altar. It was on the candle and my memories that my focus had been centred as I sat alone in the chapel, not on the structure of the building.

I was about to say, 'Small wonder that this is what he picked up on'.

But it isn't a small wonder. The whole subject, really, is a huge wonder.

***

This incident raised further questions for us about how remote viewing worked. Was this Einstein's 'spooky action at a distance'? It certainly has a spooky element to it, but we were eager to understand more. In order to explore further, Asher hit upon a new idea. He embarked on some solo RV attempts, to check whether a human subject needed to be present at the site to be viewed and whether other factors affected the success rate. His planning and the care he took to explore as systematically and logically as he could showed how he had matured since his early experiments with dowsing, for example. His claims of success erred very much on the side of caution, rather than being extravagant and unproven.

The results were fascinating. He found he could indeed view places remotely without another person being *in situ*, but the success rate varied greatly depending on whether the place he viewed was of particular interest or significance to him; if, in his words, there were enough 'energies' to link him to the place. Those *energies*, he decided, were the critical factor. They could, as we had learned, come from a person he knew well being in the location and giving him an energetic anchor of some sort, but they could also, he now discovered, emanate from other sources.

Here is part of his written account of these experiments:

***

The idea of selecting a location to view myself and using Google to verify results occurred to me. I selected the names of a variety of different places which I know exist but I do not believe I have been to and although I can't rule out the possibility of having seen images of them before, I have at least no conscious recollection of doing so.

I generally try for specific railway stations, bus stations, libraries and high streets/town squares.

For railway stations I've had quite a good success rate. I try to describe features like number of platforms, colours, decorations, the degree of modernness, ticket office size/design and sometimes have success with surrounding scenery and the position of roads, car parks and taxi ranks.

I know some would argue railway stations are much the same from one to another and their features largely dictated by the size of the area they serve, but I think my degree of detail and accuracy in some cases goes beyond that sort of logic. I am also aware that I have had an extensive amount of experience with rail travels. However, I think that links in with the energies thing.

***

His degree of clarity when viewing bus stations was markedly weaker than for his beloved railways. As he pointed out:

***

my experience of bus travel is substantially less than that of rail and the success rate isn't as good as with railway stations which I think is further evidence of the energy thing.

***

The hit rate with high streets or town squares, he rated 'OK'. This, he decided, was partly because although he found towns interesting, they lacked the strong energetic link he needed to lock on to them and partly because numerous town centres were very similar and often lacked many distinguishing features.

Libraries came lowest in his proportion of successful viewings. There was an exception, however.

***

I think there has only been one good success and while libraries have never been somewhere I have frequented, the particular library in question is somewhere I frequently send parcels to as part of my job, which I think is evidence of the energies thing.

***

After a year or two of focus on remote viewing, there seemed to be little else to discover. Ash had hoped that the accuracy and detail of his viewings would continue to improve with time and practice, but it appeared we had reached the limits of our success and that all was dependent on the strength of the energetic link he could forge with the target.

Having read a fair amount of literature on various scientific experiments related to psi abilities, I've noted that there is almost always a falling off of successful results over time, as the people being tested lose motivation and interest in an activity they have repeated on many occasions. Further evidence of the 'energies thing', perhaps?

Asher continued to use his remote viewing skill from time to time, when he could see value or an advantage in doing so, but our weekly sessions dwindled.

Once more, he retreated into near silence and eventually told me he was no longer interested in pursuing any more psychic explorations. After six months or so had passed, if I asked him about something we had previously discussed, he would tell me he had no memory of any of our esoteric conversations or experiments.

I felt puzzled and disappointed but decided, sadly, as I had back when he was sixteen, that our 'secret life' had probably run its course. I resolved to carry on alone, reading and pondering on this amazing world that the boy who had shown me his 'map of all the atoms in the universe' had opened up for me. I continued to care and wonder about him, to send him friendly messages and to hope that things might change, but for four long years there was no contact from Asher beyond a monosyllabic text once a week to let me know he was still 'fine'. Suggestions to meet up or chat by phone were politely declined.

There seemed to be no way back this time. I was certain that our story had ended.

Once again, though, I was entirely wrong. Asher was still exploring, but in a very different way, and once we were both ready, he would be keen to share his new discoveries with me.

Part IV

Asher Explaining

***

As will become clear, the material in this final section often strays into metaphysical regions where concepts such as 'consciousness' are used. Asher would argue that there are too many ideas to be fitted into the straitjacket of that single word. Throughout this part of the book, I've therefore used an upper case C to refer to the overarching universal 'force of nature', while an individual's own personal consciousness keeps the lower case 'c'. Hopefully, that will go some way towards satisfying him.

Chapter 15

The Empty Ink Bottle

Perhaps you will recall, much further back in our story, my conversations with Sarah and John and the spirit guides Sarah was able to channel. I had never forgotten their advice: to speak to the almost silent Asher in my mind and trust what came back to me in reply.

It is that word 'trust' which holds the key. It's one of those nebulous concepts like 'faith'. It sounds so simple and straightforward, but everything logical in my head was screaming that it didn't work for me. Naturally, I often spoke to Ash in my mind. I wished him well, I hoped he was happy, I told him I was here if he ever needed me, I asked whether anything was worrying him and, above all, I asked why he had cut his communication with me to the barest minimum and apparently closed down all the psychic skills that had been such a huge part of his life. That was the easy part. Then I tried to clear my mind and wait for a response.

Nothing.

Well, almost nothing.

Was there some sort of a message trying to come through? Sometimes I almost felt there was, but usually I dismissed it instantly as wishful thinking or delusion.

And then a day came. It was a miserable, cold, wet December morning and my mood matched the weather absolutely. I was remembering Asher and wishing with all my heart that I could speak with him again — real, meaningful discussions. I was sure there was so much more to talk about. Why didn't the elders' advice work for me? What about that telepathy they'd insisted was coming?

Then a thought struck me. I could try using a method that had worked for me before. Hadn't Asher once told me that using crystals and dowsing would enhance someone's psychic ability?

I went to find my beloved crystal dowsing pendulum, the very one I'd used so many years earlier to pick up messages from Nina, Asher's mother. I sat at my laptop and typed. I wrote down all the feelings that had been brimming up inside me: my memories of the fun Ash and I had had riding around in trains discussing metaphysics, the long, rambling phone conversations and the astonishing remote viewing experiments, my frustration at the lack of progress with telepathic communication and my ardent wish to find a way to resume our conversations. Then I pressed caps lock and return. With one hand I held the pendulum so that it settled over the centre of the keyboard. I focused on holding it quite still. Just as it had done all those years before, it began to move, swinging left and right, forwards and backwards and pausing to circle over one letter and then another. With my free hand I typed each letter the pendulum stopped at. Just as it had done with Nina, the pendulum gave a second rotation at the end of each word. When the communication was over, the pendulum just kept swinging around in a wide circle.

Quite simply, the message that came was this:

FEEL INTO MY HEART

Gently, I put the pendulum down and closed my eyes. I waited quietly to see what images would come as I wondered what was in Asher's heart. Very clearly, I saw a grey stone floor and a cold bench, also made of stone. There was a small window, high on a wall, with the sky visible. The word 'dreams' came into my mind. Next I was aware of a table. On it were a notebook and pen — an old fashioned pen, the kind that had to be dipped into ink every few words. There was an ink bottle, but it was empty. Now I could feel an urgent longing coming to me from Asher. He wanted me to fill that bottle. He wanted me to give him the ink so that his words could flow.

When the image faded, I opened my eyes, turned to the keyboard and typed the impressions I had seen and felt. Once more I picked up the pendulum and dowsed for a response.

DO IT

So where did those words come from? *Was* it a delusion? I'd clearly been feeling very down that day, yet the images I got as I obeyed the dowsed instruction and felt my way into Asher's heart were so vivid. Could it be a message from him? The peremptory instruction seemed to be very much in keeping with his tone when he was impatient and waiting for me to catch up. The trust still wasn't fully there, but this time there was far more than a glimmer of hope.

Perhaps, as a reader who has come with me this far on my journey, you are wondering why I was so doubtful. I had, after all, experienced the telepathic contact with Asher and with several of the children in that remarkable class. I knew I'd been able to communicate with his mother in spirit and I had been party to his remote viewing and other ways of using consciousness. This, though, was different. It bothered me because it didn't work the way our telepathy had before.

*****

This is how it used to be: I clearly remember a Sunday afternoon, when Ash was about sixteen. I had been sitting at my computer, engrossed in preparing lessons for the following week, when I was suddenly overcome by a feeling of intense anxiety. It was so pervasive that I actually got up and went to check that all my family were safe and happy. That was when I realised the sensation must be coming from Asher. I phoned him.

Immediately he answered, with the words, "You took your time!"

He had taken it for granted that I would receive the feeling he was sending to me telepathically and would call to find out what was the matter. Well yes, he could have just phoned *me*, and I told him so. His reply was that this way was better. He went on to explain that he had a work placement interview the next day and was concerned about it. Once I had run him through a mock interview and given him a few pointers, the anxiety left both of us.

***

So yes, telepathy *had* always worked between us, but the sender had been *aware* of the sending. It had been, as I saw it, fully conscious and intentional. Now, though, when I messaged him and asked whether he had been contacting me telepathically, he ignored my questions. I tried sending him transcripts of our dowsed conversations. These too were ignored. If I asked point blank whether he had been aware of them, he said he hadn't. So I had a dilemma. The telepathic messages that were reaching me had his personality stamped all over them. The conversation flowed more freely as each day passed. There was a maturity and a freedom to express himself that had been lacking earlier in his life. The neuroses and the agonising over word choices had gone, but then this was not a *verbal* conversation. It was, as he put it, a conversation in his 'first language': telepathy. He was able to project his thoughts to me and I was able to turn those thoughts into words. I was providing the ink for his pen!

'Trust what you are given', that channel had told me. I didn't begin to understand, but the clearer and more fascinating the communications became, the more I trusted. The messages came regularly. After a few weeks I was advised to put the pendulum aside (I invariably 'knew' what he was conveying before beginning to dowse anyway) and to sit away from the computer with a notebook and pen. I received ideas, images, responses to my questions and instructions directly in my mind. One of those was very insistent: I must write this book!

Patiently, I explained all this to the physical and still fairly uncommunicative Asher who lived in London. Still he denied all knowledge of it. It was with considerable trepidation that I told him his 'telepathic self' wanted me to turn his thoughts into words and to gather them together with my reminiscences in a book about our life together. I explained that I would need his permission to do so.

How many times had I broached that subject? How many times had he refused to allow it? Yet suddenly, despite claiming not to be aware of what some other aspect of his consciousness was up to, he agreed. As long as I changed all the names and avoided details that would identify him as the subject, he gave me his blessing. Despite his physical self's denials, it seemed there was some contact and awareness there.

***

Surely, though, there needs to be some reason I am able to receive these telepathic communications, which do not seem to be commonplace in our world. When I consider this, I am forced to believe that, as Asher stated at the beginning of this book, we pre-plan our lives in some way. At a higher level of awareness, the two of us *intended* to meet in this lifetime, each carrying or acquiring the requisite skills to communicate using this method. Asher has honed the ability to slip beyond his body and to gain knowledge from The Realms. He arrived on the planet (as perhaps we all do in our earliest stages of life) with telepathy as his first language and showed a marked resistance to putting it aside. He used it to great effect in the class where we first met. For my part, I had always been open to the possibility of learning from the children I taught. Perhaps that, along with a willingness to embrace the unconventional, was why I was able to tune in to my students' telepathic messages back then, while other adults in the classroom remained oblivious to them. That was my 'trigger point', I believe. Those children somehow sensitised me to this ability. More steps had to fall into place, though, before this present level of communication could take place. Asher needed to develop a working understanding of the language of spoken and written words. I needed more years to master the core skill of every educator — the ability to translate complex ideas into simple language. Only once all this had been achieved were we ready to commence our very special dialogue. Not only is it an effective way of sharing information from The Realms, it also clears a path for others to follow, should they wish to.

***

It might be helpful to allow 'telepathic Asher' to explain why he feels this book needs to be written. What follows came the day after he had delivered what I considered to be an astounding piece on the nature of consciousness.

A: I feel excited. We are starting to have the sort of conversations I'd dreamed we would and you are recording them so that they can be shared with others.

J: You said a while back that what I wrote wasn't to be just a book of wise words, as the world already has enough books like that, but when you deliver material like last night's, I'm not so sure!

*A: But the point is, that wasn't just me. The whole is more than the sum of its parts. It's the synergy between the two of us that makes this happen. In a sense, you are playing a part in guiding me to explore particular avenues of discovery. Sometimes you ask me specific questions, but even when you don't, there is a level of communication coming from you that suggests certain directions. I can best describe it as a merged curiosity. **That** is what I want to get across to people.*

This isn't channelling and it isn't just a dialogue. It's something new, but there are others who can achieve it.

It is almost impossible for one individual to be able to move beyond the physical enough to reach deeply into Consciousness, while remaining grounded enough to able to explain it in human terms. I can have the knowledge and awareness as I journey alone but I need help to bring it 'down to earth'. As you share our story, others like you will acknowledge the wisdom and knowing they have seen in children or adults they care for or guide. There are people like me who 'live in the clouds' but can't function on the ground well enough to tell their own stories. However, they will have that one person they are aligned with who will be able to blend consciousness with them and bring the story back.

J: I suppose there must have been countless individuals who had access to wisdom they could not put across to others; maybe countless parents and teachers who, like me, knew they had a specially gifted person in their lives but felt that nobody would believe them if they spoke about it.

A: Yes. There have been many and there are many now in our world. We owe it to them to share our story so that they will gain the courage to speak out and form the kind of alliance you and I have made.

***

Ash clearly has a very definite idea of his target audience. For him it is important for those who, like him, struggle to share their 'knowing' with people they care about, to be given a voice, or metaphorical ink for their pens. However, there is a wider sweep of humanity he also wishes to reach. The following words arrived directly and forcibly in my mind from him one evening:

A: People want someone to show them 'Heaven'. Many are disillusioned with religions because the rituals have become dissociated from their original purpose and the gods have been turned into *parodies of humans. They're disillusioned with most of the scientists because they **know** there is more than the physical universe and the scientists deny that. Many people know their 'dead' relatives are still around; they know it doesn't all stop here. They want it explained, but they want some intellect in there, not just cosy stories.*

***

This final section of the book, then, is largely a collection of Asher's 'knowing', interspersed with comments, questions, prods and gasps of surprise from myself.

The 'intellect' he promised is present, and as he has used my memories of scientific or philosophical books, articles and lectures as a background from time to time; there may be the occasional reference some readers will want to look up.

If you are curious to know more about the Realms he visits, the wisdom he has gained and the discoveries he has made there, read on.

Chapter 16

Astral Envelopes

One of the most astonishing and effective techniques we have established in our telepathic communication is what we term an 'astral envelope'. It works rather like the writing desk and ink-bottle image. Asher will send these when he has a long and complex message of particular importance to convey.

I am told to leave my pen and book aside, close my eyes, relax, take several deep breaths, yawn a few times and wait to see what arrives. In some magical way, subtle but definite concepts and sensations reach my mind, which duly translates them into emotions, thoughts, movements and images I can understand. I often get a straining or prickling feeling at my brow chakra or 'third eye' at such times. When the 'mind movie' is over, I record my impressions in the notebook and Asher helps me to interpret them, where necessary.

One evening, not long after our regular telepathy sessions had started, Ash sent me an astral envelope without giving any hint beforehand of the subject matter. What I felt and saw was as follows:

First there was a profoundly deep sadness and regret because something was breaking down. It appeared to me as a great tree, dying and falling to the ground. I felt sorrow for the tree, but at the same time I experienced it as if I *was* the tree. There was a strong, crushing feeling as it/I moved lower and lower, until it sunk deep into the earth, below the forest floor. Once the tree had gone, there was nothing but a clear space. Everything was calm then. There were no more feelings, just a world without the tree. A few birds came and pecked around and I was wondering whether there had been any point in the tree having been there. After a while, there was a pulsing or breathing sensation, almost as if someone was blowing life/prana into the area around my heart. This pulsing vitality rose in an arc, like the sun rising. Then there was another (or the same?) tree standing huge, with vibrant, golden yellow leaves in the sunlight.

The image faded and I returned to my notebook, recording what I'd felt and sharing it with Asher. He was delighted with the result, telling me I had picked up his concepts very clearly and saying he liked the way I'd interpreted it as a tree, because that worked well.

I was confused, asking whether I'd been shown some sort of circle of life and death, which didn't really seem to fit, or whether there was a more specific meaning.

This is how he explained what I had experienced:

A: I wanted to show you what life was like for me when I could no longer stand tall and work with you.

I believed, in equal measure, that I was able to access The Realms and that I was sick and delusional. It simply became impossible for me to maintain these two opposing views of myself. For years — since my teens — I'd been swapping between the two, but finally the split became inevitable. I doubted all the wisdom I 'knew' and wrote. I couldn't take the strain of that and needed to release it and let it sink into the ground.

*My physical self let the spiritual side fall away. It was then, as you saw, as if this aspect of me had never been there. This part of me is **dead** to my physical self. 'He' is now free to live the life 'he' chose — narrow and repetitive but manageable.*

*Next there was a period of adjustment. Remember, we are not our bodies. This non-physical part of myself was able sit **in** the body, making sure it had the energy it needed to manage life comfortably.*

Then you saw some new strength coming to me. I can't explain exactly what the Light is, but there was a surge of energy at my heart. There was no conversation, of course, but if there had been, some benign force would have told me that if I elected to leave the physical *self in that low-energy state, the remaining consciousness had work to do. The second tree you saw — the golden yellow one — was this non-physical aspect of me. You can call it ephemeral but it is as real, in fact **more** real, than the physical self. The Light reminded me who I am. That's what it does.*

***

Well over a century before this incident, the American psychologist and philosopher William James commented that our normal waking state is only one particular type of consciousness. He spoke of how 'the flimsiest of screens' separates it from other, quite different, forms of consciousness. Asher, it became clear, had travelled beyond that screen.

As we continued our telepathic discussions, Ash couldn't grasp why I found his 'separation' so difficult to understand. He pointed out that at night each of us leaves our body more or less immobilised in bed, yet with enough residual consciousness to breathe, to digest, to age and to be able, for example, to roll over without smothering itself in a pillow, whilst the remainder of our consciousness is experiencing an alternative reality in the dream state. He insists that his own separation works in a similar way, although it is more permanent.

He asked that I continue to send friendly phone messages to his physical counterpart, but not bother that aspect of him with questions or requests to resume any of our previous activities, because he would no longer be able to recall them. I agreed to do that, sad to have such minimal contact with the young man I'd once known so well, but excited to discover what his non-physical self had to teach me.

To begin with, I was curious to know what had been happening during those four years of silence.

A: For a while I just inhabited my physical body and didn't have to think much.

J: So that's the point, in the astral envelope you sent me, when the tree had gone, the ground was barren and nothing mattered. A few blades of grass grew, but mostly nothing.

A: That's exactly how it was. The trouble was, I just went numb. It became a habit.

J: That was what I found so hard to understand. You'd been such a curious, open-minded person and suddenly you just stopped doing anything.

A: I know. It didn't do my psyche any good, I just sank into lethargy.

J: You showed me that a new 'tree' grew from your heart and the 'Light' had to come back.

A: Yes, that's what happened. I left the body to go through the motions of living its daily life and I worked at the level of my mind/ consciousness beyond the physical. It felt like climbing. I just got on, searching out the truth of how things work. It was lonely and tough but I needed to do it. I had some innate knowledge, but it was like having a few pieces of a puzzle and having to discover the rest so that I'd be able to see the whole picture. In the end I made a lot of progress.

J: Clearly you did. You have far more advanced perception now.

***

I asked if Ash would be able to send me another astral envelope to show what his exploration of The Realms had been like, once he had made the breakthrough. Remember that the concepts he sends are interpreted by my mind as a set of mental images. Some aspects may be lost in translation, but I seemed to get the gist here.

At first I felt that my head stayed quite still and focused in a single direction, but I was somehow able to look right around — through 360 degrees. Next I was flying like a drone very fast over familiar English landscapes. I came to a curtain or veil and knew I had to rip it to move beyond. At that point I felt I was going so deep into the 'envelope' I was virtually asleep. I saw a book behind the curtain. My mind viewed it like something from a Harry Potter film: a massive magic book with writing that appeared as light shining out of the pages. I recognised that Asher wasn't reading the words, he was absorbing the light, so that it flowed into him.

When I described what I'd seen, he told me that was a suitable way of visualising it.

A: I was given access to all the information I had wanted. Once I got 'there' (although it isn't a physical place, of course), it was quite effortless. I could just drink it all in.

J: I think you were accessing that material in your early teens.

A: Yes, I was, but then it was involuntary. I would just spontaneously get fragments. This time, after I'd done the 'work', I could control it. I could find out what I wanted to know.

J: That must have felt amazing.

A: It did, but I missed having you to share it with. I had all this knowledge but there was nothing I could do with it by myself.

J: So you were quite alone? No guides or energy forms or anything?

A: No, that's right. It was like winning the lottery and not being able to spend the money. I saw the potential for sharing it with other humans. The world was in such a mess. So many people believed they stopped at their bodies and I was barely using mine. It all felt wrong.

J: Couldn't you have linked back to your body? Then you could have told me.

A: No. The rift between my physical self and my mind/consciousness was too deep. I did keep trying to reach you telepathically but you didn't pick it up for a long time.

***

Asher went on to explain how his 'subt nav', the subtle light navigation discussed in Part One, drew him towards finding a way to link back to me, so that I could work with him. That was where the book-writing would come in. It would be the way to 'ground' his knowledge. I, too, of course, as described in the previous chapter, was being nudged by my own 'subt nav' to search out a way to link to him.

Despite the unconventionality of this method of contact, it works surprisingly well and easily for both of us. He is delighted to be able to communicate directly with me, freed from the restraints of physicality. I thoroughly enjoy being able to resume our fascinating discussions, and at a far more complex level than before.

Since Asher is keen to reach out to others who have the potential to engage in a dialogue like ours, or who are already doing so but fear ridicule if they discuss it, the next chapter will provide more detail on how telepathy works.

Chapter 17

Trains of Thought

Imagine a bubble or a cloud, suspended somewhere above you. Once you can picture it, you can send your thoughts there. If you have a close connection to another human being — twin, parent, child, partner, close friend — that person may be able to send their thoughts there too. That 'communication bubble' is where the exchange of information takes place telepathically. That's roughly how Asher explained the process to me. It seems to be linked in some way to what scientists refer to as quantum entanglement, in which it has been shown that two or more particles are able to exist in a shared, or 'entangled', state and continue to retain information about each other, regardless of how far apart they are. The deep reality implied by this finding gives us a very different worldview to the one we normally understand in everyday terms: a world in which telepathic communication exists.

A: This link we have during telepathy is purely at the level of thought. The aspect of you that connects to me is beyond the visible body. It is at the vibration of thought. The fact that you are physically aware of it, though, and consciously writing it down means that I put ideas into the bubble and you find and 'wordise' them — turn them into words.

We have slightly different ways of approaching the telepathy. I am actively searching your mind for suitable thoughts, memories and ideas to help form the images I send to you. You are talking to me in your mind, waiting for what comes and quickly recording it in your notebook.

***

Although much of our communication is experienced and recorded here as dialogue, there are times when our thoughts become so blurred that it's impossible to say which of us is 'speaking' and which is 'listening'. The two somehow blend into a single thought or what Asher terms 'a merged curiosity'.

As the months have passed, I've noticed that while at most times I am in contact purely with what Ash calls his 'telepathic self', there seem to be times when his physical self tunes in and joins, or at least is somewhat aware of, the discussion. There are also instances when I am aware of, and doing my best to write down, a conversation that my physical self is *not* involved in. I become witness to a discussion between his telepathic self and my own. It has taken me some time to adjust to the way 'non-local' communication works.

If this is all starting to sound far too complex, I'm glad to say that Asher holds on to his human awareness and has a gift for finding just the right analogy to make the material easier to understand. He has made it very clear that a telepathic self is not the same as a higher self or soul, existing beyond the human framework and looking down on it from 'on high'. He may usually be out of body, but he's still the same Ash. It took me ages to understand that, so he gave me the following explanation, making use of his enduring love of trains, which shows how close he still is to his human personality:

A: I'm not encumbered by a body or time or space, so in that sense I am free to follow any 'train of thought' I want.

J: I don't know if the answer is quantifiable, but to what extent are you Asher and to what extent are you Spirit or pure Consciousness?

A: Don't think either/or — think AND! If you can imagine the light body as a spectrum of light stretching between the core of the earth and the Realms, I'm a train of thought on the Asher Line. You're on the Jes Line.

As he worked through this analogy, Ash made reference to a railway line we were both very familiar with — the one we had travelled together so many times when he was a boy — between Bellington (not its real name) and London. It is a busy commuter line and operates both express and stopping trains on parallel tracks.

Asher uses Bellington to represent the start of the line (our physical selves) and London to represent The Realms. He has picked a station halfway between them, which we will call Stanebridge, as the point where our telepathic bubble is located.

A: My train, travelling on the Asher Line, has run over some faulty points. Some of its carriages have become uncoupled from the rest. Let's say this problem happened near Stanebridge. My train can still travel between London and Stanebridge and carry my passengers (thoughts) on that part of the line. However I can't get them to Bellington.

Your train is running on the Jes Line. It runs parallel to mine. If my thoughts/passengers want to reach Bellington, they can — with a certain degree of difficulty — get out of my train at Stanebridge, move across the track and make their way on to your train, which will convey them safely to their destination.

Because my train can't jump across to your line, it has to keep travelling between Stanebridge and London, collecting more passengers, while you shuttle them along your clear line to Bellington.

The points on my track have a habit of malfunctioning. Still, as you head for Bellington you can wave to my separated carriages!

J: Indeed. I'll say 'Hi' to them for you.

***

That final point was, of course, a reminder that he wished me to stay in contact with his physical self — the abandoned carriages.

Asher's references to the faulty railway track points and their tendency to malfunction are a way of acknowledging his neurodiversity: the autistic spectrum perception which causes/allows him to function differently to the majority of the population. We have had many telepathic discussions on how life on the autistic spectrum differs from the 'neurotypical' and these will be covered in their own chapter.

As I have already said, I am an avid reader and since our telepathy sessions started, I have been searching books for material that will help me to understand telepathy better, from a human perspective.

Eventually I came across the writings of Alice Bailey who was active in the early decades of the twentieth century. As I explored her work, I found that most of her books had been dictated telepathically by a Tibetan 'master of wisdom' who wished, for his own reasons, to remain anonymous. Well, there seemed to be a certain synchronicity there, so I decided my 'subt nav' must be guiding me to study her work more closely. Alice wrote many books and I admit my studies have been fairly basic, but from what I can work out, she suggests that there are various levels of telepathy. As I summarised them, Asher agreed that they fitted well with our experiences over the years we've been working together.

The most basic level is described as sending **negative** emotions to the target. This seems to manifest as 'gut feelings', because it comes from and travels to the solar plexus area (centre of body, stomach). That, when I thought about it, was exactly what I experienced back in our classroom, when I sensed little Jimmy 'beaming' his frustration at me because he wanted help with his maths. It's also what Ash used to do when he sent feelings of anxiety to me across town, rather than pick up his phone and ask for help with a problem, such as how to deal with that interview.

The next of Alice's levels is centred on the heart. As one would expect, it is similar to the first, except that **positive** emotions are sent and sensed by the receiver. This is a rush of warmth, love or happiness from someone you are connected to. There have been times when I've sent Asher a positive text message and some time later felt his pleasure as he picked it up. If I looked at my watch when the telepathic feeling arrived, it invariably matched the time he had checked his phone.

Moving up the body, the next major chakra point is the throat. This is where Alice Bailey says the 'intellectual' level is located. This involves people sending word messages to one another via telepathy. As I read her description, I recognised that this was what I'd seen that group of little children doing in the school garden, so many years ago: conveying information to each other without actually speaking the words.

Asher had some interesting comments when I told him about this.

A: Yes, that's accurate. You and the other staff were working to activate our speech, so everything was centred on the throat. We children were, in a way, testing the speech muscles at an etheric level, before using them in the physical body.

J: That makes sense. It's what your young friend Max used with me so effectively. I could feel his voice in my mind. At times it seems to be what you and I do, particularly if you need to send me a word that's unfamiliar to me. I somehow perceive how it sounds, even if I can't spell it.

*A: Yes, we do use that at times. I mean I **have** words and I can use them if it's the only way to get my message across. It's just that I see words in little boxes — tight, limited things. I feel frustrated if I have to use them. Most of the time I have a more fluid, more expansive range of thought strategies open to me. The word use overlaps with the other stages, though, in the same way that physical conversation makes use of emotional voice tones, expressions, gestures or imagery.*

Alice's final level of telepathy is called 'intuitional' and works through the brow chakra, or 'third eye'. She seems to be saying that this transfers concepts as instant downloads and in the form of pictures. Asher readily agreed that this was what we use most of the time in our communications, particularly, of course, with the astral envelopes.

***

I will finish this chapter on how our telepathy works with another of Asher's rather ingenious analogies. It also, in places, gives an example of the thought blending that takes place when we are on the same wavelength.

J: Is there a way you can make clear to me what is happening to make your thoughts appear in my mind and to make mine appear in yours?

A: I can try. Let's see. To begin with, as you write your words in that book or wherever you write them, they become thoughts. You think them as well as writing them. Is that clear?

J: Yes.

*A: So thoughts **exist**. They have energy and existence. Think of them like droplets of water released into the atmosphere.*

J: OK, I like that analogy. To me they vanish as if they evaporated but they are still there and you can 'condense' and receive them in your mental state. Is that it?

A: You know what you did there, don't you?

J: I read your thoughts! I read them without you 'thinking' them to me in this turn-taking form.

A: YES!

J: So I feel as if I'm on the brink of understanding something big now. I assume there needs to be a certain 'directedness' in the thoughts. I mean presumably you don't pick up every thought I have; just the ones aimed at you?

A: Yes, and vice-versa.

J: And now you're going to tell me that we can still have conversations outside of time: your response to a question or comment from me does not need to follow it in temporal terms.

A: Exactly. You're doing well.

J: I'm getting it theoretically, but not in terms of my own 3D logic. I mean, I know about things happening outside of time order from some of our remote viewing activities and from my reading of Dean Radin's experiments with 'retro causality' (events being influenced mentally after they occur) but even the scientists don't get how it works. Any more handy analogies?

A: Stay with the water droplets. You aimed them at me and I was able to condense and see them; I had a metaphorical cold pane of glass to catch them on.

J: Yes, OK. I get that.

A: There isn't a 'when' for that to happen. They're there in the atmosphere and I can catch them at any point. I simply have to intend to retrieve them.

J: Yep. Got that, I think. So what next?

A: 'Next' I have reciprocal thoughts: replies to your comment or question and I send those back to you. More water droplets.

J: OK. And do I have a cold pane of glass too?

A: Yes. You have the ability to receive my thoughts telepathically.

J: Right. Yes, but I'm firmly stuck in time.

A: Well, that's not a problem. Thought is timeless, so you pick mine up whenever it's comfortable or convenient for you to do so. My mind finds and responds to your ideas regardless of what my physical body is doing.

***

So, although I find it mind-bending to try to understand that our conversations take place in a dimension where time has no sway — that, for example, Asher could answer questions I've yet to think of — I now have some grasp of the process involved. Most importantly, it works and I feel confident to share the wisdom and knowledge I am picking up in this way.

Chapter 18

The Realms

I'm continuing this journey into our telepathic connection by asking Ash to explain what he perceives these Realms he visits to be. From his assertion as a teenager that there were 'no words' that could describe them, I knew this would not be an easy task, but I've done my best to record the ideas he sends to me.

The first conversation here is rather abstract, but as we have discussed it further, Asher has found various analogies to make it a little clearer.

*A: The Realms are a kind of psychological landscape. They are composed of light vibration. This is difficult to describe in human terms because we are not talking about **places**. Basically, there is nowhere and 'no-when' that is not enfolded and unfolded, formed and informed by The Realms.*

Scientists would call it a non-local field. That doesn't mean it's far away. It means it has no physical location. When you read your science books they use many different terms to label it.

J: Yes, I've seen it described as the Zero Point Field, The Field, Akashic Realms, Electromagnetic Field, Morphic Fields, Implicate Order, to name but a few.

A: It seems the people who coined those terms discovered its existence through maths and the sciences. There are many ways to access The Realms, though. Once the scientific study of such phenomena becomes mainstream, more people will be able to expand their perception enough to travel mentally to The Realms, which will give them a way to utilise powers such as psi abilities.

When I asked him to describe The Realms, the first image he showed me was of a great Tudor library with bookcases ranging from floor to ceiling. I was slightly surprised by this idea, so he explained:

A: When I was a small child in your class, you took us on an outing to an old mansion. I'd never been in a place like that before. There was a huge library and it really impressed me. That memory stayed in my mind, and yours, so that is the image I have used to convey the bays in this bank of knowledge in The Realms. Some people might see it as a collection of scrolls or sheets of parchment, but that doesn't matter. We all access it in our own ways.

That made it easier for me to understand, but I couldn't get any clarification from him on the word 'bays' — one he often uses when he is accessing information. I was imagining something like bay windows, which didn't seem to fit with the image he'd sent me of displays of books ranged along the walls of a Tudor library.

As I've mentioned before, I sometimes worry that I'm drawing on my own imagination, rather than receiving material directly from the mind of Asher, as the communication is so subtle. This, though, was certainly not a word I would have dreamed up in this context. Feeling puzzled, I decided to hunt for an explanation in another source, so I grabbed my phone and typed into a search engine, 'What is the meaning of "bays" in a library?'

Instantly, the following words appeared from Wikipedia:

'A bay is **a basic unit of library shelving**. Bays are bookcases about 3 feet (0.9 m) wide, arranged together in rows.'

Ah!

In all the countless hours I had spent in libraries over my lifetime, including two jobs as a school librarian, I had never known that those vertical sections of shelving had a particular name, far less that they were known as 'bays'! I felt rather embarrassed by this gap in my knowledge, but considerably encouraged that I was indeed picking up Asher's messages accurately. He, after all, works in a large academic institution, so probably uses the word routinely. As can be seen in the following discussion, it's exactly the right word in the context of what he is describing.

J: Can you explain what it is like for you when you travel in The Realms?

A: OK. The 'place' where I access knowledge is a massive bank of information. In human terms it would be called endless, but it's also 'beginningless' because there is no space or dimensions — more like cyberspace in that respect.

There are bays. I know that seems to contradict what I just said, but if I want to find a particular piece of information, I put out the intention to know whatever it is and instantly the most relevant bay is in front of me. That's because there are many nuances or variations in the type of information I might need and I therefore have a selection to refer to, to find exactly the part I need.

There is guidance. I'm drawn more towards certain parts than others, but I have the option to move on to different sections of the bay if I feel they would broaden my knowledge.

J: So rather like Googling?

A: Far more subtle and instant, but there are similarities. That's not just coincidence, by the way. As humans open more to Light/ Spirit, they are inspired to create information systems that resemble the records I can reach.

J: You mentioned guidance. Some sort of librarian?

A: That's the nearest human equivalent, or an extremely sensitive and empathic search engine. It's a subtle nudging that suggests very gently that a particular 'text' may be what I need.

J: And I'm guessing that you absorb the information instantly, the way you did when you used to lay your hand on books and know all that they contained.

A: Yes, that's right.

J: I assume this is what is known by some as the Akashic Records.

A: I suspect it is, yes.

***

I pointed out that not all his 'travelling' seemed to have been to these bays filled with infinite amounts of wisdom and knowledge. I recalled times, particularly during his troubled adolescent years, when he had mentioned visiting what he then called 'the plazas'. I'd found his descriptions of these to be quite threatening and uncomfortable. Would he, I wondered, be prepared to explain that aspect of The Realms?

A: Although The Realms are not physical places, it may help to think of them as if there were different levels. The emotional state of the traveller will determine the 'level' he or she will discover there, so someone who is in a 'dark place' mentally and/or psychologically will find themselves in a similarly dark environment there. What I call the plazas are a shadowy and uncomfortable 'place' where those who wish to escape physical life, but have not shaken off the heavy energy, will congregate. It isn't a matter of there being a 'Heaven' and 'Hell' in the traditional sense of those words, but The Realms will reflect our own psychological state and allow us to explore it and hopefully find a way to reach a more comfortable level.

***

How and why that little boy who so effectively grabbed my attention all those years ago should grow up to have such abilities is quite beyond my comprehension, but as I said at the outset, I am by nature an extremely curious person and I set about asking him to hunt through this inexhaustible library he has access to, to answer many of the questions I have been unable to find responses to from earthly sources. The subject of the next chapter presents one of the most vexing questions for modern day scientists and philosophers alike.

Chapter 19

Where Is Consciousness?

Having read so many books and articles filled with opposing ideas on what science calls 'the hard problem of consciousness' — some claiming it resides firmly inside the human brain while others insist it exists both within and beyond the body — I was keen to understand Asher's grasp of this subject. It turned out to be something he had studied in great depth and was happy to discuss.

Note that in the dialogue below Asher refers at times to 'in-formation'. This is a concept we have borrowed from the ideas of scientist and philosopher Ervin Laszlo, to stress that there is a dynamic and constantly developing nature to the material accessed by the human brain. It is, at once, in formation and information.

My initial question was, simply, "What exactly are mind, brain and consciousness?"

A: You know what brain is. It's the primary interface with the mind, but they are not synonymous. The mind interpenetrates the physical body but exists beyond it, too. As you and I have these telepathic communications, they are mind-to-mind. I'm not using my brain. You are using yours to transfer our thoughts into words and record them with your pen on paper, but we can still converse if you put those aside. Agreed?

J: Yes, certainly. I see the difference in those terms, as when you place a concept or image directly into my mind. I 'know' it before I begin to think about how I will write it down.

A: The mind delivers 'knowing' from the 'in-formation field' of The Realms to the human brain while we are physically alive and aware. The brain picks it up as sensory perceptions, and processes it to make deductions, suppositions, choices and creations. It's as if the mind is delivering a pile of Lego bricks and it's down to the brain to decide what to make of them. Each person will examine the bricks they have and identify the ways they could fit together. They'll also imagine and hypothesise what to make with them.

J: You're identifying the respective tasks carried out by the two hemispheres of the brain, there.

A: Yes. There are links being forged between those two sides and the more a person examines and considers, the more rigorous and complex and valuable those links become. This is learning and creating: brain work. It's very different from the 'knowing' the mind has access to.

In our particular case, I am very proficient at the logistics — delivering vast quantities of bricks. You have an advanced skill in building models from that raw material. You interpret and process it. That's why I spend a lot of time out of my body and you stay firmly embedded in yours. Helpful?

J: Extremely. Can you explain where intuition fits in? I was listening to a talk by a neuroscience researcher who claimed that intuition is in the right hemisphere of the brain. Is it?

A: I'd suggest he is mistaken. To ascribe a location in the body for intuition is very simplistic.

J: I'm struggling with it. I don't see intuition arriving with the cart-load of Lego bricks. Oh! Unless it's the little instruction booklet that comes with them...

A: Be careful not to push the analogy too far. Intuition is not a set of instructions. It could be viewed more like an open-ended idea sheet with a few hints and tips. The brain can ignore them. We all have free choice, remember. In fact, it's very important that the brain does the creating. That's why we incarnated in 3D reality. Whatever is created in this world expands the in-formation field. The mind of an individual is an information exchange, maybe like a bank: paying in or withdrawing, with information being the currency.

J: Yes, that works. So I am depositing ideas and experiences in this in-formation field and receiving 'knowing' from it. It strikes me that

I would probably not always be aware of the latter, except as sudden 'subt nav' nudges or thoughts 'out of the blue'.

A: Yes, people largely don't know what they're engaging in, but when they say they need to mull something over or go away and think it through, that is the process. The mind takes the specific idea from the brain and places it into the in-formation field, while also drawing out useful knowing to augment it. In a very real sense, our brains are expanding Consciousness.

J: Ah, so we've reached consciousness now. Are you able to define that for me?

A: I can't give you a definition of consciousness because everything IS consciousness; there's nothing Consciousness isn't.

J: I can get that theoretically, but it's hard to grasp how it all works.

A: You know I find words restricting, but if we take the underlying concepts, it would be misleading to equate consciousness with sentience, which commonly happens when people speak about something being 'conscious' or not.

J: So consciousness is everywhere, but sentience is restricted to the 'knowing' and 'brain work' that you have been explaining?

A: Yes. Consciousness is overlaid with the ever-expanding in-formation field. It's expanding because it's constantly in formation. See how dynamic that is?

J: Yes, I do.

*A: As I said, **everything** is Consciousness. Your entity, at root, is consciousness. It is energy with intention. If it helps, we can envisage consciousness as fractal, so it's there at every scale from the overarching All-That-Is, to a single quark or electron. In terms of human beings, we have the subjective consciousness of an individuated self and a wider group/collective consciousness which defines the perceptions of a society/tribe/family.*

J: Can we explore those 'subjective consciousnesses'? I presume they are what an individual person would see as their own personal consciousness. Are they just a very small fractal part of the overarching

Consciousness, or is there something intrinsically different about them?

A: You know what I'm going to reply to that!

J: You're going to say, "Not OR, but AND."

A: That's right, but then you will say, "So that means there is something intrinsically different about subjective consciousness."

J: Yes! But I'm picking up that there are certain differences at every scale. After all, fractal means 'self-similar', not 'self-identical'.

A: That's very relevant. I suspect people tune into the perceived differences at this scale in particular because we are quite invested in being human. We think about it a lot. Each person believes they are separate from the rest. In 3D terms, they are, but at a cosmic scale, everything, and everyone, is Consciousness.

***

I was still interested to learn more about consciousness in human terms. Asher therefore asked whether I believed I was incarnate. When I responded that I certainly did, I was asked to look at that word more deeply.

J: In-carnate: basically the word means 'in meat'. I believe that I am currently in flesh and bone, so in a 'meat suit'; that is, being a physical human.

A: Yes. So if 'you' are dressed in this meat suit of yours, what, exactly, is the 'you' who has put it on?

J: Ah. That must be consciousness then...?

*A: We'll call it a light body. Envision a pillar of light that extends from the highest source (zero point field, All That Is, Akashic Realms, Source, or what you will) to the depths of the earth. This is your light body. It is made of Light. It vibrates at different frequencies from very high to very low. The part of it that interpenetrates your physical body vibrates within the **visible light spectrum** — the part of light you can see with human eyes.*

J: It sounds as if you're talking about chakras. Violet at the top of the skull, red at the base of the spine and the other colours ranged between them.

A: Yes, in a way, but it's more accurate to visualise the colour flowing through it, blending gradually from one to the next, the way colours merge in a rainbow. Focusing just on the chakras gives a limited grasp of your full creativity. Imagine red light from the base flowing up and gradually becoming more orangey until you reach the sacral chakra, where you hit pure orange, then as the light carries on it gets more yellowy until you're at the solar plexus and so on.

Ultraviolet is above the human head, although those people who are receptive enough to sense it will view it as white. You've also heard of an 'earth star' chakra beneath the feet which is described as being black. In fact it is infrared. Your human body covers only a small part of your entire light body.

This changed much that I'd previously been taught about the body's chakra system. I asked Ash what the advantage would be of thinking of the light within the body as a gradation of colour, rather than separate chakra points.

A: You'd be utilising your entire available light body. Imagine having a box of 100 coloured pencils but only ever using seven of them — adequate but limited. Using all the shades you become 'lighter' and more able to flow. I think you need to meditate and experience it to know what I mean.

***

I was still keen to discover what part consciousness played in all this and how it interacted with the human brain. Ash assured me that consciousness could leave the physical body, but not this 'light body' which interpenetrated it. He reminded me that I had heard of 'altered states' of consciousness, which were measured in brainwaves.

J: Oh, you mean like Alpha and Beta and Theta and all that? I've read that there are very calm, deep states of meditation and, at the opposite end of the scale, extreme anxiety and panic.

A: Yes, but what the scientists measure are the levels of consciousness **interacting with the body**, *because they can't measure what is non-local. It's like they are measuring shadows and mistaking them for the actual consciousness.*

J: You mean the EEG brainwaves are a measure of how much of a person's consciousness is lodged in the brain?

A: Yes. Find and copy one of their charts showing brain states.

I found the following information, which I copied into the notebook.

***

Beta (14–30Hz) awake and alert

Alpha (9–13Hz) relaxed and drowsy

Delta (less than 4Hz) deep sleep

Theta (4–8Hz) sleep with dreams

Gamma (more than 30Hz) heightened awareness

***

If it's possible to receive a snort of frustration telepathically, that's what came to me next! Asher took what I can best describe as a deep breath and suggested I reorder those brain states in order of frequency. (Hz apparently means cycles per second.) He then agreed to tell me what was really happening at each of them.

Here is what he gave me:

***

DELTA: *Consciousness is not centred in the body. Body is alive but dormant/unconscious, so it could be in a trance, in what scientists call* 'deep sleep', in a coma, under anaesthesia, injured or having a near death experience.

THETA: Transitional state between being conscious and unconscious. Dreaming or in a hypnagogic state just before dreaming, meditating or sedated.

ALPHA: The physical body is relaxed, calm but fully conscious. Tuned in to intuition ('subt nav') but also grounded.

BETA: The state in which most humans stay on a daily basis — more tuned in to day-to-day physical life, problem-solving, coping with stresses and strains yet sometimes noticing synchronicities or having flashes of insight that help them cope.

GAMMA: Hyper-vigilant and very aroused. This could be a reaction to fear, excitement or stress: pumped up, fight or flight, panic attack and so on.

***

J: Interesting. Thank you. So that is a measure of **brain** activity, not consciousness activity?

A: Yes. That's important. To scientists, almost nothing seems to be happening in Delta, but that is where **consciousness** is at its most expanded. At the other end, in Gamma, where they are picking up frenetic brainwave activity, the person's consciousness is barely in touch with anything beyond the physical body. It's not tuning in to synchronicities or the higher self. It's working with nothing more than physical sensations. That's **not** how humans are designed to work. It's exhausting and unproductive. The whole point of being **incarnate** is linking the soul self into a human body while retaining links to the spirit realms.

J: So to get out of Gamma we need to breathe slowly or follow other relaxation techniques to slow us down and connect back to the helpful 'subt nav'?

A: Yes, but of course there are times when Gamma is necessary. If you're being chased by a bear, meditation is not going to help. You *need your whole consciousness to be in the body to help you escape. The problems come when humans spend long periods of time in artificially induced Gamma states. They can get stuck there.*

J: You're talking about adrenalin junkies, people addicted to exciting video games or to recreational drugs?

A: Yes. The conscious awareness can get trapped in the physical body because the body fears it can't manage without it.

***

As I was trying to grasp this download of information, Asher did something new. He directed me to draw a diagram. Under his instruction I drew a human figure with a cone-like funnel shape coming into the head from above and narrowing to form a channel through the whole head and torso, then opening out into a second identical funnel shape around the legs and down into the ground. When I had finished, he continued,

A: That's it. You have drawn the physical body interpenetrated by the light body. Remember the light body extends above and below the human one. Your diagram shows total balance — Alpha — which is the optimum state for human/spiritual development. The light body is fully grounded and linked to the earth and also open to higher Consciousness, in that it links to the soul, higher self and beyond.

In Theta it's not so balanced. The cone of light would be wider above the body and narrower below. That means the person would be less grounded and more in touch with the higher realms. Consciousness is more focused on soul than on the physical.

In Delta, consciousness has left the body in a dormant state and is in the higher realms completely: 'out of body'.

Now consider what the changes would be if you move from Alpha to Beta.

J: I suspect it's the opposite to Theta, unbalanced in that it's more focused on the earth and less aware of the higher realms. Concerned

much more with the physical. The upper cone would be narrower and the lower one wider.

A: Exactly. But in Gamma, imagine two trap doors being pulled across — one at the base of the spine and one at the crown of the head. It's as much a 'catastrophe' for the physical body as Delta, but in a different way. The physical body clings on to the consciousness in its part of the light body, in order to manage its extreme state of arousal in terms of sensory input. It severs its links to earth, so is not grounded in physical reality. That means it can't use 'common sense' or relate to other people, places or fellow creatures. Its outlook (or 'inlook', basically) is caught up in the self. It has also severed all connections to higher frequencies. It can use consciousness within the brain to react and deal instinctively with problems and sensations but has no recourse to intuition, 'sixth sense' or even to memories of how it has coped with similar situations in the past. The consciousness trapped in the brain can respond only to sensory data, which it analyses in great detail ('overthinking'). That adds to the sensory overload, of course.

✱✱✱

Of all the information Asher has given me over the years, I have found this the most life-changing and fascinating. It is, of course, a million miles away from the 'brain training' and business-based emphasis on being more productive by encouraging Beta and even Gamma states. It is equally different from the New Age concept of doing one's best whenever possible to drift out of physical consciousness into 'higher' altered states.

All the brain states, obviously, have their purpose, but Asher is insistent that during our time as human beings, we should aim to maintain a balanced Alpha state, in which we are equally aware of our subtle-light navigation system of intuitions, inklings and synchronicities and of the instincts, memories and sensory support we receive from the earth when fully grounded.

***

To finish this chapter, I'll add the help Asher gave me when I asked him to explain, in layman's terms, what being 'grounded' actually involved. I'd heard many gurus talking vaguely about 'being in touch with the Mother' or 'breathing in energy from Gaia' and not found that particularly helpful.

Here is Asher's straightforward version:

A: Being grounded is easiest to imagine if you think of an animal. Wild creatures are fully grounded. They are of the earth. They make good use of their physical senses and of 'feedback' from the planet. They live according to their physical needs and urges; they rest when they are tired, seek food when they need to — to eat or to store, they use daylight and darkness, heat and cold, sun, wind and rain so that they can be in tune with their environment and care for their bodies. There is a part of them that is alert even in sleep, unless they can safely hibernate. It is difficult to be grounded inside a building or in front of a screen. Walking, sitting or standing in the countryside, amongst trees or beside water is the best way to achieve this state.

Chapter 20

Two Tribes

There was something that didn't quite fit in all the talk about consciousness. It had been nagging at the back of my mind for quite a while, and never more so than after Asher had given me the information in the previous chapter.

As a teacher, tutor and mentor, I had spent much of my life working with children and young people who could be classified as 'neurodivergent'/'neurodiverse' (as opposed to neurotypical). Most literature on the subject lumps together those diagnosed with various syndromes, disorders and conditions, including autistic spectrum perception, under this banner and for the purposes of this chapter, I will use these as convenient, though very generalised, terms.

***

As I read back through the description of the Delta down to Gamma states Ash had provided, it occurred to me that very few of the neurodivergent (ND) people I have known and worked with seemed to spend much — if any — time in the Beta brain state, despite Asher's assertion that this is the state in which most people spend the majority of their daily lives. I also had a suspicion that ND people were probably more familiar with Theta than the neurotypical (NT) population.

So I researched it. Sure enough, scientists have discovered that many ND people tested with EEGs have 'abnormally' low activity in Beta and correspondingly high activity with Theta waves. The testers (predictably) saw this as a defect that needed to be cured. Some also noted Gamma 'spikes' in the Theta brain state.

When I explored spiritual, rather than medical sources, Theta was explained as the state at which ideas, insights, creativity, intuition and high levels of productivity took place. It was also, interestingly, mentioned as the ideal state in which to engage in remote viewing.

I put all that to Asher and his response was that my suspicions and research had been spot on. He explained that when he had given me the original brain states/consciousness information, he had aimed it at the neurotypical population as that seemed a logical starting point. In typical Asher fashion, he had then waited for me to notice that the ND population was different. When I asked for information about these differences, I was told it was ready and waiting.

***

Here, then, is Ash's description of the five brain states as experienced by the neurodiverse population:

DELTA: This is still the state in which consciousness has left the physical body. It is a state the ND mind enjoys and aspires to for short periods of time because ND people enjoy that level of connection with Source and expansion. Many discover ways to go out of body, such as astral flying.

THETA: For most ND individuals this is the 'at rest' state. It requires some connection to the physical world but the way consciousness functions in this state feels most natural. Tools such as synchronicity, insight and 'just knowing' feel appropriate for gaining knowledge and creating solutions. At this level remote viewing or mind-reading can happen pretty spontaneously.

*ALPHA: As mentioned before, this is the optimum state for humans, but just as NT people have to make some effort to 'reach up' to this level, NDs have to make a similar degree of effort to step **down** to it. It involves being equally open to Spirit and earth, so to become more grounded than people are in the Theta state. However ND people* *can achieve this state and thus connection to the planet, its locations and habitats as well as to animals and other people. Always, though, in Alpha there is a balance and even earthly things are seen from a more spiritual perspective.*

BETA: This state is extremely difficult for the ND brain and is avoided or not achieved. Although a link remains to higher levels in Beta, this is not enough to allow the ND individual to process and cope with the dense physical data. It feels like quicksand: intensely uncomfortable and very hard to negotiate. Confusing.

GAMMA: Because of the pressure from NTs, who are currently dominant on earth, ND people will often enter this state through fear or anxiety. It is a reaction to the attempts to force them to cope with Beta. It can also be self-inflicted — an attempt to 'fit in' with the NT way of being. The Gamma state blocks out all but the current 3D moment. There is no access to resources beyond the physical body's limits so the consciousness simply goes over and over whatever stimuli have caused the initial anxiety. It can result in meltdowns, panic attacks or self-induced isolation and a sense of being frozen. (I was given an image of a deer caught in car headlights and frozen in fear there.)

***

That seemed to tally well with what I knew of the way Asher had always functioned, as well as many of the others I'd worked with who had autistic spectrum perception.

Next I asked about the 'geekiness' and laser-like focus on small detail that is a feature of many in the ND population. Ash explained that this was a way of attempting to hold their consciousness in the 3D world and to survive with relative safety when having to navigate the Beta state. As a rule, ND people are easily overwhelmed by sensory data in the 'everyday' world, so they will often narrow their focus to particular 'nerdy' areas of study or minority interests, which they can comfortably pursue, often in isolation or small, like-minded groups.

***

Despite having known many people with autistic spectrum perception — including Ash himself, of course — there was so much I didn't understand about the differences between ND and NT individuals and whether they had any bearing on Asher's rather specialised perceptual abilities.

J: I'd like to grasp what makes some people 'special' and how the 'normal' ones like me fit in with them. I've read articles saying that ND perception allows people to have paranormal skills, but I notice that many ND people have no apparent interest in the kind of work you do.

A: Imagine a bunch of people standing in a street. They are scattered about and some are definitely over on the left side while others are on the right. There are some pretty close to the middle but who just fall on the left or right. So let's say the further left you are, the more you will be perceived as neurodivergent and the more to the right of the road, the more you will present as neurotypical. The people in the central area won't seem very different from one another. We have talked before about how ND people differ from the norm: the 'cracked vessels' you saw them as, letting in Light to the world through those cracks, the tendency to live in a Theta rather than a Beta brain state and being less 'grounded' in everyday life.

*As well as that natural 'way of being', though, there needs to be a desire, in a free choice sense, to engage with consciousness beyond the body. That is **not** dependent on how ND or NT a person is. You, for example, are neurotypical but have a strong wish to 're-member' your link to Spirit while staying grounded.*

J: So do ND people have more potential than the rest for going to your 'library' and connecting to The Realms and their spiritual side, even though some choose not to?

A: Yes. They have a clearer channel to Spirit available to them than the NT population. It is natural to them to 'know' instinctively rather than by laboriously acquiring knowledge through study.

However, pressure from NTs and the low self-esteem they feel from being made to feel different and inferior can influence them to shut the connection out, in the way that a small child might stop believing in an 'imaginary' friend she sees and talks to if adults repeatedly tell her she is lying or pretending.

***

These telepathic dialogues make it far easier for Asher to explain how human life feels from an autistic-spectrum perspective than had been possible when he was communicating with me through speech or written word alone. He clearly values the opportunity to do this.

One evening, he asked a deceptively simple question…

A: What does a mirror enable you to do?

J: To observe my own outer appearance; to let me see myself as others see me, although I think we often don't see ourselves the way others do, because we filter what we see with our own prejudices.

A: Interesting. So if others don't see what you do, what do they see?

J: They have filters too — their own prejudices about others. When people love someone, they see them 'rose-tinted', in soft focus. If they dislike someone, their perception accentuates the unpleasant things. If meeting someone new, they judge them by first impressions. It must be different for autistic people, though. You don't perceive body language and facial expressions the way NT people do.

*A: No, we don't. As a human, I look **into** people. It's like glass. You can look at it or through it. Other people appear like that for an ND person. If they say one thing but are feeling another, we are aware of that and it's confusing.*

I thought back to a four-year-old I once worked with. Jethro was a highly sensitive little person and definitely belonged to the neurodivergent population. One day he had a quarrel with his best friend and came to me in floods of tears.

"She said she was sorry," he told me through his sobbing, his eyes wide and uncomprehending, "but I looked into her heart and that wasn't what was there".

Thinking about it, I suppose that's why I've tended to get on well with autistic children and young people. I learned to be authentic. There was no point in lying or pretending because they'd spot it at once. No one ever explained that to me; I just came to recognise it as I worked with them.

***

Another aspect of ND behaviour I'd seen was the problem many had with words, whether spoken, heard or written. Asher gave me this:

A: When I and some other ND people produce sound, it does not come easily. To others it seems discordant. Words are a kind of 'freezing' of ideas and sounds into symbols. For that reason they can create a barrier or problem for some ND people. When we try to speak, we must consider volume, pitch, tone, expression and intention in order to communicate verbally, as well as creating the actual sounds with breath, mouth and throat. These things are exhausting and difficult. It is such a crude method of communicating compared to telepathy! After all, we usually know what others are thinking. It would be so much easier if they could feel our thoughts.

Of course, when people who are used to speaking and writing their thoughts enter the Theta state, they realise their experiences can't be verbalized in any useful way. They say such things are ineffable. For me, so much of my experience is ineffable. That's why I don't speak much.

***

Working on this section of the book with Ash has given me a far better understanding of how neurodiversity in general, and autistic spectrum perception in particular, feels for those who are experiencing life that way. One day, though, I was reading an article on artificial intelligence written by a sociologist. The author claimed that making sense of our environment, of the meaning behind words, expression and social behaviour was one of the main elements of being human, as opposed to AI. Feeling saddened by that point of view, I asked for Asher's thoughts on that.

A: I'd say the writer has a limited grasp of what 'human-ness' involves. Like many NT thinkers, this person equates neurotypical behaviour with human, and neurodiverse with imperfect human. It's a very chauvinistic way of thinking — similar to the way men used to think women were inferior because they differed from themselves in certain ways.

J: Yes, I agree completely. What 'knowing' do you now have about neurodiversity that can help us explain that those like you are more than AI in skin-suits?

A: As I've said before, neurodiversity covers a very wide range — far wider, of course, than the neurotypical population. ND broadens the bandwidth of what is possible for humans. It extends in every direction. That's not to say it always leads to superhuman abilities or cognitive brilliance. The ND person may appear very limited in accepted terms, but I think the multidimensional nature of their experience is of interest.

J: So the neurotypical population at large appreciates the wider perspective of the ND high achievers — Albert Einstein, Steve Jobs, Nikola Tesla and so forth — but may see most neurodivergent people as failures with faulty bodies and minds. Do those labelled with syndromes and disorders all have 'secret lives' and other types of consciousness?

A: Each neurodiverse individual is different and has their own special reason for incarnating in that ND body. There is no overarching general way of being, but you are right that each is exploring life in a different way to what presents as physical limitations.

***

I've been struck again and again, while working in this way with Asher, by the care he takes not to make generalisations and to acknowledge the free choice and individuality of all people experiencing life on this planet.

The aim in this chapter has been to suggest that normality doesn't exist, except in the eye of the beholder, but that humanity does have a fairly fuzzy dividing line between two 'ways of being'. I hope that comes across.

Chapter 21

Creation

Ash was keen to share what he understands of how events and objects on earth are created. He started in an unusual way — asking me to seek and write down impressions from my own 'telepathic self' rather than interpreting thoughts he sent to me, as I usually do. He was there to encourage me gently to ease myself further into it, 'like putting on a comfortable pair of shoes'.

I felt that I was on the verge of falling asleep as the images came but Ash assured me that was useful, because it prevented my logical mind from filtering and potentially altering the information. This is what emerged:

*J: I'm getting a single, finite event, like a sort of pillar or monument with things splintering off from it. Now I'm getting the word 'dents'. I don't know why. To me the pillar has apparent solidity. It represents an irrefutable event — perhaps something in the mass consciousness. But... Oh! It's not splintering but being **formed** by individuals. The separate minds are creating it: putting it together from their personal realities, so although it looks to be an object in its own right, it's an amalgam of all of our views. Am I being told to look for dents, the imperfections or anomalies that show it is a composite of all our ideas?*

A: It's both forming and disintegrating. The event comes together as a mass creation but it will then immediately start to splinter off in different directions. Imagine a thousand people all bringing their own thoughts to a point where they coalesce into a 'thing'. For that moment in time, that thing is a collective creation and they all share it, but it can only exist in that form for that moment — like grains of damp sand pressed together to make a shape. After that created moment, each person will move on with their personal subjective impression of the thing/event and that changes it. The grains of sand fall away and each person takes their own memory of it on into their life. Each will have a different memory.

J: That's the clearest explanation of 3D reality I've ever heard. Is there a difference between events and objects though? Events occur in time, but objects are in space as well: the World Cup Final as opposed to the Houses of Parliament.

*A: Yes, objects have more permanence, but they are changing — cracking, weathering, moving and so on. It is the **creation** that has the energy. The object is just a memory of the initial creative event.*

***

Ever since Asher first demonstrated how to create an outcome through focus and intention, back when he was a boy in that train carriage with the bottle of water, I have been hoping for a full explanation of what happened.

Of course, there are many books on manifesting in the mind/body/spirit section of any bookshop or library which insist that purely forming the intention and having faith is enough to produce magical events. Books in other sections will insist that such things are coincidence at best and charlatanism at worst. Thankfully, from my perspective, Ash seeks to explain the way in which 'creation' occurs on a daily basis in a careful and thorough way that manages to incorporate aspects of magic and science.

I asked for his perspective on how we manifest or change events and here is the discussion that followed:

*A: It has to do with that higher dimension beyond 3D that isn't time or space. Don't try to imagine it; just accept that it exists. We'll call it 4D for the sake of simplicity. So in 4D, **all** potentials exist. They can be in past, present or future in our terms because it's not temporal. Imagine that you can reach into that 4D and select an outcome of your choice. It doesn't have to follow any of the 3D rules*

— just as cubes don't have to be flat just because the 2D plane is. Still with me?

J: Yes, I am.

A: Good. So once you have selected the outcome or event or object, you can take it out of 4D and overlay it on 3D, just as you could take a face from a 3D cube and overlay it on a 2D square.

J: Right, I've got the theory. How can it be achieved in practice?

A: It's like with the bottle: **See it where you want it to be.** *Visualise, with all the clarity and intention you can, the outcome: where and how you want it to be. You will reach a point where it becomes inevitable that the event* **must** *happen, because you have overlaid it on the grid of all potential events. Because this is the event that now has the focus, that is where the strings of intermediate events leading up to it will go.*

As I sat with my notebook, writing those words down, I was aware of an image forming clearly in my mind. I imagined a flat sheet of thin rubber, from a child's balloon, perhaps, stretched over a frame and held taut. If I poured water on to it, the water would splash about and might end up anywhere. However, I saw that if I placed a pebble at a place of my choosing on the sheet of rubber, there would be a dip, caused by the weight of the stone. Now if I poured water on to the rubber surface, it would all run to that point. Ash was delighted when I shared that idea with him.

A: Absolutely right. You are starting to get my messages in thoughts and images at times, rather than words.

J: So you didn't send that analogy?

A: No, but I sent the concept/idea that you received and interpreted in your way, first in words, and then your mind found a clearer way to show you the idea.

J: So once I had put the pebble (intention) in place, I would have no doubts about the water (string of intervening events) flowing towards it, because it couldn't do otherwise. That's the certainty you were describing.

A: That's right. You're less familiar with working in a 4D environment, while living in 3D, so you fear that you don't have the skills you need, but of course you do.

***

Now I had the theory, but it was still sounding rather like one of those MBS books I mentioned. Asher had not finished, though. First, he gave detailed suggestions for how to practise this way of creating reality, just as we might use physical exercises to develop muscle strength in the body. After that, he linked this information with quantum physics, in ways I could never have imagined.

First his suggestions on how to learn to create one's experiences:

A: Perhaps the easiest way to explain is to say that every person in physical 'reality' is a magician. Each of us is able to work with consciousness (4D) and actively create what will show up in life. Because people are largely unaware of this, they will need some practice.

*It is fairly simple to put energy into creating a small event, so over a period of a few days, give as much energy as you can to believing a certain small object will show up in a familiar place. Make it something easy like a leaf, a feather, a spider or a coin. **Expect** it to appear and wonder how long it might take to turn up. When it does, congratulate yourself and be assured that it was the energy you put in which caused it to enter your life.*

Next, try the reverse: cause something to disappear. Remember what I did with the queue in the buffet car of the train that day? That's a good exercise to start with. Think of a place you need to go: a shop, a ticket office or a petrol station, for example. Picture yourself going there and as you do so, focus on there being plenty of space in front of you. Put all your energy into the idea of emptiness and spaciousness.

If your mind is conjuring up people, just imagine them wandering away, leaving a wide space. When you have that image very clearly, it's time to go there. Don't make the mistake of sabotaging your efforts by thinking, 'Huh, no way this will work, there's always a queue', because of course if you do that, your energy is creating a queue in your reality.

The process, either of moving an object into a space or of emptying a space is not at all difficult. It's how your consciousness works. The difficult part is allowing yourself to believe it, because you have thousands of years of conditioning to get rid of. That's why I suggested starting small, to build up your belief in your skills.

Some people instinctively know these things are possible but they believe it comes about due to lucky charms, talismans or some kind of special object or ritual. Life for them works out well if they rub their lucky penny or hold their special crystal or whatever. There's nothing wrong with that except that they're not recognising their own power.

I do understand that people have been taught to believe that life is random or that 'God gives and God takes away' or other ways of existing and, of course, it's quite possible to live a life like that, just allowing it to unfold in a random fashion, but it's far more enjoyable and easy when you get used to living 'on purpose'.

I asked how this way of creating our experience would work for a person living mostly in the Gamma brain state we had discussed earlier — the highly aroused fight or flight mentality. Was it possible for them to create their experiences?

A: Because the Gamma state relies purely on responses to immediate sensory input, the degree of choice and intention isn't there. However, the basic process still exists, so if the individual's focus is on, for example, big, threatening guys turning up in their life, those guys will keep coming, because that is where the person's energy is. So yes, it still works in Gamma but not in a helpful or beneficial way.

***

As Asher said at the beginning of this section of the book, we are aiming to reach a wide and varied readership. Some people will be wondering how these 'magical' concepts fit in with hard-nosed scientific fact. Others will have little or no interest in or knowledge of science, beyond a few memories of biology or chemistry lessons at school. If you are one of this latter group, feel free to skip the rest of this chapter.

If, like me, you lack much scientific understanding but are keen to grasp how it links to what Asher has shared thus far, it would be an idea to familiarise yourself with a famous experiment which was first performed over 200 years ago and has been worked on and refined ever since. It is called the double-slit experiment and there are many articles and videos available online which seek to explain it in layman's terms. My personal favourite is Dr Fred Alan Wolf's 'Dr Quantum' animated presentation. I think it would be wise for inquisitive readers to refer to such a source before reading on, rather than for me to attempt a faulty and incomplete explanation.

So, for anyone previously or newly acquainted with the issues quantum physicists have been exploring in terms of waves and particles, here is what Asher had to say on the subject:

A: At the quantum level, scientists are exploring elementary — incredibly small — bits of stuff. We have already looked at how we use focus and intention to create and alter our lives, to shape matter from the vibrational (4D) realm of Consciousness.

J: So are you saying that all possibilities are there while the photon is in the vibrational frequency — behaving as a wave — but that the wave function collapses when it is observed, so that the superposition (which is all possibilities) becomes one single particle on one particular trajectory?

A: Yes, correct, because the event has become subjective. An outcome was expected, so an outcome — one of the many possible outcomes — had to occur. The other possible outcomes faded from the... realms of possibility. They cannot exist in the subjective experience of the observer because that would violate the rules of 3D life.

J: Like your example of only one of six possible faces of a 3D cube being able to exist in a flat, two dimensional plane.

A: Quite. It's not the collapsing of the wave function that is remarkable in that experiment; it's the fact that the wave function has been rumbled! Waves are vibrational — 4D — so quantum physics is dealing with formation of matter at such an elementary level that they are observing how our physical lives themselves are created.

*There is **always** superposition, at every level of scale. Each action has a variety of possible outcomes and by observing or participating, we are constantly (intentionally or by default) selecting **one** of those possibilities and allowing the rest to fall away. They cease to be observable since subjectivity (3D life) only permits a single outcome.*

*J: I'm actually getting this. It's like only being able to see what blood cells do because we have microscopes, otherwise we'd be oblivious to them. Going so much further down to the scale of particles — photons etc. — we can see how creation works. But then, of course, we'd have to accept that **we** are the creators.*

*A: Yes! Absolutely! Let's take a human. Call him Fred. Fred basically exists in a vibrational cosmos. There is this endless ocean of possible events, all in superposition. Fred is **conscious**, so wherever he puts his attention, there are vibrational waves collapsing and particles of a very elementary nature are being 'formed', in that Fred is creating his subjective experience. Fred's world is constantly in formation. What he is creating, as thinkers such as David Bohm, Karl Pribram, Ervin Laszlo and others have seen, is **information**. That information both informs 3D 'reality' — our individual and collective experience — and informs the Consciousness that is the zero point field or whatever you want to call The Realms.*

That, of course, is the source of all the information Asher is able to retrieve and share from his 'bays of books' within the Akashic Records, as well as the source of all those nudges, hints and inspirations we receive via our 'subtle light navigation system'. That constant addition of each new thought and concept from every conscious being, Ash assures me, is how the cosmos continues to expand.

***

I find such discussions and revelations as this from Asher very exciting. However, as he pointed out to me, neither of us has a background in science and we can expect fair criticism from those who do once we step into their territory. I am reasonably comfortable conveying his insights and perceptions from The Realms here, but there are times when our telepathic discussions stray into pure conjecture. I'll finish this chapter with one of those, but not without noting that this is not based on any more than speculation.

We discussed all those *potential* events, objects or actions that cannot exist in our physical lives once the wave of superposition has collapsed and a particular course has been selected (the equivalent of a huge number of probable but unformed particles in the double-slit experiment going through the other opening or hitting the metal plate and bouncing back off it at all possible angles). Could they, we wondered, make up what scientists call 'anti-matter' or even the mysterious 'dark matter' that forms over 80% of the universe? Something to ponder, perhaps. Asher has yet to discover any such information in The Realms.

Creation and the formation of truth go on.

Chapter 22

Life, Death and ... Carnations

One night, just as our usual evening telepathic discussion was drawing to a close, I asked whether Ash had anything else to say. His simple reply startled me slightly:

A: You are on your final chapter of the book. The material on death, life and reincarnation is the last piece the book needs, apart from the ending we have already prepared.

Well, I knew it had to end somewhere. As I sit at my laptop, I'm surrounded by eight notebooks, each filled with my hastily scrawled records of the 'conversations' we have had over the past two and three-quarter years. A few months ago, Asher helped me select which parts should be included in this volume and, as I look back, I can see that all but one of those have been covered. The final point in his list was stated as follows:

A: I suppose we need to put in some stuff about death and the way it fits into life. In fact, maybe we need to look at that next.

It was a subject we had touched on many times, but his explanation that evening, and in the two or three that followed, showed 'Telepathic Asher' at his most enthralling.

A: It would be glib to say that it doesn't matter because people don't really die. That's why I needed to have a very close, personal experience of death at such an early age — so that I was aware of the enduring pain. Otherwise I might have been tempted to trivialise it.

I've spoken before about how a human life is rather like the Self putting on a costume and acting out a part in a play. Of course, the Self is everlasting, while these lives we put on only last for a relatively short time. The thing is, I don't want to sound trite or patronising, because when people act in a play, they are pretending. They can certainly get engrossed, but not completely immersed in the experience, to the point where they forget their true personality. That's what we do when our greater Selves are living a life, though. We have a very real experience and very real emotions. Even when some of us are able to stand back and remember our wider understanding and even other lifetimes, that still doesn't stop the issues and challenges in this lifetime from affecting us deeply. They **are** real.

When a person finishes this lifetime and returns to spirit, they can remove their main focus from the physical life that has ended. I mean, they are no longer working to complete the life, because they have done that. Even in spirit, though, they retain links to the people they were with — the ones who are mourning and missing them.

J: I've often wondered about that. Almost everyone seems to have times when they feel or sense the presence of a departed loved one, rather like the telepathic connection we have.

A: It manifests in different ways. Some people have sensory experiences with the astral body; they may smell the person's perfume, hear them humming or whistling a familiar tune, see them sitting in a chair or even be aware of pictures or images. People in spirit can direct their loved ones' attention to an object or image in their environment that will have meaning.

J: Some relatives of mine saw a lorry with their grandmother's first name in huge letters on the side, while they were driving to her funeral.

A: Yes. The more people accept that such things are possible and true, the easier it will be for those connections to be recognised and facilitated. The departed want to ease the pain of separation for those they have left here.

J: So there is a desire to tell people still living on earth that their consciousness has survived death and is still going strong?

A: Yes. We are making a very valuable collection as we live our various lives. Each incarnation remains a part of us, so that when we are in spirit, we can dip into any of the lives we have lived and connect to them. I'm trying to find a way to explain it. It's as if you still had a key to every house you have ever lived in and, when you wanted to, *you could go back, unlock the door and spend some time in that house, looking at the memories and experiences and connecting with those who shared your life at that point.*

J: Yes, that analogy works. There are some old homes I have no particular connection to at this point, but others I still feel very close to.

A: I think there are better ways to explain these ideas. Maybe they will come to us as we discuss it further.

I was interested to know how, when people are able to have contact with someone who has passed into spirit — via the services of a spiritual medium perhaps — the personality seems familiar, although the departed person has apparently had many different incarnations and so, presumably, different personalities.

A: When the consciousness is no longer tied to a body, it moves into non-locality, so no time or space to limit it. The being can travel via thought — its own or someone else's. People can summon those who have left and ask them to be in contact at thought level. The personality is not the whole Self, but it can be put on again, like a costume. Once we have chosen and lived in that costume, we can (in spirit) wear it again when we choose. Imagine a whole wardrobe full of 'costumes', each a different incarnation personality. I'm not talking just about the appearance, but about the persona.

You are, in a sense, living all your lives in an eternal 'now'. A 'life plan' can remain in place through several lifetimes. The Self may see that it can be of service or help to those it had 'contracts' with. Perhaps there is a longing to do more in that contract. My mother, for example, had entrusted me to your care, but she returned in spirit to help you through a particularly tough spell.

J: Yes, that makes perfect sense. Do you have awareness of other 'afterlife' experiences?

A: I can express it only as extreme freedom. I feel freer when I separate from my body, but it is not a complete separation in the way that death would be. I still have ties and responsibilities to my physical

body. After the life is finished, returning is optional and doesn't limit
the Self.

***

Much of our next telepathic session was taken up with a
fascinating discussion of how people — living people on earth,
this time — can sometimes pick up feelings from each other,
despite being separated by miles. I'm including part of it here
as it links to the subtle ways in which we humans are sometimes
able to sense experiences beyond our 'normal' functioning. I
spoke of changes in mood I had sensed in Asher's physical self
that day. He agreed that I had picked up the changes accurately
and continued:

A: As for the 'bit' of us that sends and receives such messages,
humans have their five senses, the ones scientists can measure in
mundane ways, but the subtle senses (and yes, those are the ones I
was speaking of last night) also exist. They leave some physical traces,
change in heart rate or the skin, for example, and each person has a
set of these subtle senses. We can sense through the consciousness in
the cells of the heart or gut. With practice we can pick things up more
clearly by focusing on particular people or situations.

J: So it's like remote viewing?

A: Yes, they are related. Once, before there was language, that's
how people knew what was going on in places they couldn't physically
see or otherwise sense.

J: Yes, I understand that. Animals still have that sense well
developed, as Rupert Sheldrake has demonstrated with his studies of
dogs who know when their owners are leaving work and heading home.

***

As we finished chatting about that subject, I asked whether
Ash had got any further with finding an analogy for those in

spirit being able to access all their incarnations. I sensed the etheric equivalent of a broad grin as he placed an image into our telepathic bubble.

In my notebook, I wrote, "Oh what!? Seriously?"

Asher responded that at least it would be easy to remember and insisted that I should write it down, along with the explanation he was giving me. I couldn't decide whether it was brilliant or crazy. Ash maintained that it didn't matter, as it was just another analogy. He was clearly rather proud of it and, as we worked through the imagery, I could see his point.

As you might have guessed from this chapter's title, he had selected a flower: a carnation.

He showed the whole flower and then directed me to look into it and explore the petals. Each one, with its many twists and turns often almost doubling back on themselves, represented a single human life. Together the cluster of petals comprising the whole flower overlapped and blended one with another, showing how our various lifetimes influence and work with the rest to expand the entire Self. As spirit, he demonstrated, we had the option of delving deep into a single lifetime (petal), of exploring the connections and similarities between different 'in-carnations' in the complete flower or even of regarding a bunch of carnations, noticing how perfectly our own lives mingle and connect with others.

Final Thoughts: Truth

Some months ago, long before this book was nearing completion, my pupil-turned-teacher delivered a firm caveat which, he insisted, should be included here. It concerns truth. Asher is anxious not to come across as some kind of guru, who is sharing the answer to 'life, the universe and everything', insisting that the world has too many such people.

I hope that you have been struck, as I have, by the simple humility and honesty of this young man as he has laboured to share what he sees and discovers by the most unconventional of means. If, between us, we have expanded your world view to some degree, then this book has served its purpose.

It became obvious to me, on reading them back, that the comments at the end of the discussion below were intended to be the book's ending, so I will stop commenting here and allow this telepathic dialogue to finish twenty-five years of a more extraordinary conversation than I could ever have dreamed I might engage in.

*A: We need to make it very clear that what is written in this book is true, but not offered as 'the' truth. I search for understandings and explanations in this library of information I can reach, but **all** information is there. Every thought and idea may be found there.*

As I've said before, I do have a degree of guidance and I suspect I have a certain ability to select a set of ideas and concepts that are consistent with one another. It gives us confidence when you discover philosophers, scientists and mathematicians who have reached the same conclusions by using very different methods, but I am not claiming it as the only way things work.

After all, there are many other equally gifted philosophers, scientists and mathematicians who reach very different conclusions. That is also true of religious and spiritual teachers.

J: I can accept that there are alternative paths, but I struggle to see that certain scientific beliefs are a truth — materialist reductionism, for example: the belief that we start and end inside the physical body and that life runs like clockwork.

A: OK, let's look at 'truth' from the perspective of one of those people. He is exploring the physical world in a very specific way. He is fascinated and excited by the Newtonian 'truths' and let's face it, almost every human on the planet is living and perceiving at least the majority of their daily physical life in accordance with those laws. Our materialist is blown away by how brilliantly everything works. He can observe with powerful microscopes and telescopes and the symmetry and structures are so perfect, he can't doubt that he is seeing the truth.

J: And yet he thinks it all came about through a happy accident...

A: He has no choice but to think that. He and his kind cannot see any viable alternative. They are rational; that's the antithesis of faith and superstition. If he opens the door even a crack to such things, he fears he'll end up having to accept God.

J: Yes, I see your point. Our story, for example, hinges on the idea that 'we' are far more than the physical body and that you and I made a pre-life agreement to meet up and form this alliance. I can't prove that. I have no memory of it. I have your word, John and Sarah's channelled elders' word and my own belief and faith. Many people would reject it though.

*A: Now you can see your materialist's point of view. One day, in this life or another, he will find there is something that can't be explained by his truth. At that point, he will begin a search to incorporate that new something into his world view and **that** will result in an expansion of his viewpoint. He won't instantly abandon materialism but he will expand it and step into a new appreciation of how things work.*

J: Thank you. It gives me hope. We are all expanding, but in different ways and timeframes.

A: Exactly.

J: Maybe we need to look at what religions say about The Realms.

A: What works for us now is no more an immutable truth than what the Ancient Egyptians or Vikings believed. 'Truths' will open and close in the fabric of time.

Imagine the windows of a train carriage on a wet winter's day. They steam up and there are raindrops further obscuring the view, but every so often, a traveller will wipe a portion of the misted window with a sleeve, so that they are able to see a fairly clear view of the 'truth' outside. Of course, the train is constantly moving, so that first person's truth will be quite different from what appears to a second passenger who wipes the window when the train has moved further along on its journey. Both will be 'true', but not the same truth.

J: So it's for the truth-seekers of every generation to peer through and find the truth for their time, but just as the scientific inventions of a century ago have often been modified or surpassed, so the truths we live by will have altered.

A: Exactly. Some will always cling to the old ideas. It's never a smooth process and there will be reactionaries who refuse to change, but gradually they will be side-lined and life will move on.

The only truly timeless element of truth on earth seems to be the golden rule — treat others as you'd like to be treated. The truths and beliefs will come and go and people will always be formulating new ones and trying to make others feel bad or wrong if they don't follow them, but that in itself breaks the fundamental rule.

We are building up the information in the bays. They are constantly in formation. Every thought and idea and wish of every individual adds to it. We all have hopes and dreams and they become the common property of humanity and of the cosmos.

About the Author

In her everyday life, Jes Kerzen B Phil has enjoyed a huge variety of roles in many educational settings, from specialist speech and language teacher to head of English, from running an alternative education hub for home educated children in a mediaeval abbey undercroft to collaborating with a farmer and a life-sized model calf, while delivering workshops on social and emotional skills in rural primary schools in the west of England.

Jes always had a particular interest in working with neurodiverse students, particularly those with autistic spectrum perception and communication challenges. Life tends to give us more of what we need, so it was hardly surprising that wherever she worked, these were the children who so often appeared in her life and enriched it greatly.

Since first meeting Asher, she has spent a quarter of a century researching telepathy, remote viewing and other psychic abilities, along with the spiritual insights they can sometimes lead to. She still devotes time to working with Asher, continuing to learn from him and writing about their work together.

Jes lives in a 350 year old cottage in Somerset, in the southwest of England, and enjoys walking, gardening and having chance encounters that could lead to all manner of interesting discoveries.

A Note from the Author

Thank you for sharing our amazing journey. I hope very much that you have found *A Mind Beyond Words* intriguing and, perhaps, inspiring.

If you have a few moments, please feel free to add your review of this book to your favourite online site so that others may discover it.

***

Be assured that Asher and I are still in close contact and our work goes on.

Every weekend I 'wave to his derailed carriages', which in practical terms involves sending text messages to keep in touch with his physical self in London. He continues to send back short replies and because we are no longer able to travel on those wonderful train excursions, I often send him a short video of some interesting place I've visited.

As for 'Telepathic Asher', his explorations of The Realms continue unabated and he is still very happy to discuss them with me and to head off in search of answers to whatever comes up in that merged curiosity of ours. He has hinted several times that there will be a second book...

I'm certainly not ruling it out.

If you would like to connect or stay updated please visit my website where you will find news on any upcoming works and recent blog posts: http://www.ashertree.com.

Sincerely,

Jes Kerzen

6TH
BOOKS

ALL THINGS PARANORMAL

Investigations, explanations and deliberations on the paranormal, supernatural, explainable or unexplainable. 6th Books seeks to give answers while nourishing the soul: whether making use of the scientific model or anecdotal and fun, but always beautifully written.
Titles cover everything within parapsychology: how to, lifestyles, alternative medicine, beliefs, myths and theories.
If you have enjoyed this book, why not tell other readers by posting a review on your preferred book site?

Recent bestsellers from 6th Books are:

The Scars of Eden
Paul Wallis
How do we distinguish between our ancestors' ideas of God
and close encounters of an extraterrestrial kind?
Paperback: 978-1-78904-852-0 ebook: 978-1-78904-853-7

The Afterlife Unveiled
What the dead are telling us about their world!
Stafford Betty
What happens after we die? Spirits speaking through mediums
know, and they want us to know. This book unveils their
world...
Paperback: 978-1-84694-496-3 ebook: 978-1-84694-926-5

Harvest: The True Story of Alien Abduction
G L Davies
G. L. Davies's most-terrifying investigation yet reveals one
woman's terrifying ordeal of alien visitation, nightmarish
visions and a prophecy of destruction on a scale never before
seen in Pembrokeshire's peaceful history.
Paperback: 978-1-78904-385-3 ebook: 978-1-78904-386-0

Wisdom from the Spirit World
Carole J. Obley
What can those in spirit teach us about the enduring bond of
love, the immense power of forgiveness, discovering our life's
purpose and finding peace in a frantic world?
Paperback: 978-1-78904-302-0 ebook: 978-1-78904-303-7

Spirit Release
Sue Allen
A guide to psychic attack, curses, witchcraft, spirit attachment, possession, soul retrieval, haunting, deliverance, exorcism and more, as taught at the College of Psychic Studies.
Paperback: 978-1-84694-033-0 ebook: 978-1-84694-651-6

Advanced Psychic Development
Becky Walsh
Learn how to practise as a professional, contemporary spiritual medium.
Paperback: 978-1-84694-062-0 ebook: 978-1-78099-941-8

Where After
Mariel Forde Clarke
A journey that will compel readers to view life after death in a completely different way.
Paperback: 978-1-78904-617-5 ebook: 978-1-78904-618-2

Poltergeist! A New Investigation into Destructive Haunting
John Fraser
Is the Poltergeist "syndrome" the only type of paranormal phenomena that can really be proven?
Paperback: 978-1-78904-397-6 ebook: 978-1-78904-398-3

A Little Bigfoot: On the Hunt in Sumatra
Pat Spain
Pat Spain lost a layer of skin, pulled leeches off his nether
regions, and was violated by an Orangutan for this book
Paperback: 978-1-78904-605-2 ebook: 978-1-78904-606-9

Astral Projection Made Easy
and overcoming the fear of death
Stephanie June Sorrell
From the popular Made Easy series, Astral Projection
Made Easy helps to eliminate the fear of death through
discussion of life beyond the physical body.
Paperback: 978-1-84694-611-0 ebook: 978-1-78099-225-9

Haunted: Horror of Haverfordwest
G.L. Davies
Blissful beginnings for a young couple turn into a nightmare
after purchasing their dream home in Wales in 1989.
Paperback: 978-1-78535-843-2 ebook: 978-1-78535-844-9

Readers of ebooks can buy or view any of these bestsellers by clicking on the live link in the title. Most titles are published in paperback and as an ebook. Paperbacks are available in traditional bookshops. Both print and ebook formats are available online.

Find more titles and sign up to our readers' newsletter at
www.6th-books.com

Join the 6th books Facebook group at
6th Books The world of the Paranormal